I am My Body

I am **My Body**
Blessed Pope John Paul's Theology of the Body

Jim McManus C.Ss.R.

redemptorist
p u b l i c a t i o n s

Published by **Redemptorist Publications**
Alphonsus House, Chawton, Hampshire, GU34 3HQ UK
Tel. +44 (0)1420 88222, Fax +44 (0)1420 88805
Email rp@rpbooks.co.uk, www.rpbooks.co.uk
A Registered Charity limited by guarantee.
Registered in England 3261721.

First published April 2011

Cover and layout design by Peena Lad

ISBN 978-0-85231-387-9

The scripture quotations contained herein are from the New Jerusalem
Bible, published 1990 and copyright 1985, by Darton, Longman & Todd
Ltd and Doubleday and Company Inc., and used by permission of the
publishers.

A CIP catalogue record for this book is available from the British Library.

Printed by Joseph Ball (Printers) Ltd. Leicester LE2 5LQ

Contents

Preface

The love song is as old as human history. In every age human beings celebrated their love and their yearning for love in song and poetry, in drama and dance. As a young man Karol Wojtyla, the future Blessed Pope John Paul II, became in his turn one of the great troubadours of love. As soon as he became Pope he wrote to the Church his famous words:

> Humans cannot live without love. They remain beings that are incomprehensible for themselves, their lives are senseless, if love is not revealed to them, if they do not encounter love, if they do not experience it and make it their own, if they do not participate in it.[1]

This encyclical letter set the tone for his long years of service as Pope. His message resonated worldwide, especially in the hearts of the tens of millions of young men and women, from all cultures, and from all over the world, who flocked to hear him and to spend time in his presence. What drew them in their millions to him? It was the truth that he spoke to them. He held up before their eyes the truth of their own bodies and enabled them to see their dignity as men and women in a new and exciting way. They welcomed that revelation. They were renewed and transformed by hearing it and in their millions they have been living it.

It is Blessed John Paul's teaching that I seek to unfold in this book. His teaching is original and profound, rooted in the whole tradition of Christian faith, yet expounded with captivating new insights. I have been conducting week-long courses on John Paul's *Theology of the Body* for the past four years. I have witnessed for myself the light in the eyes of the participants as the truth summed up in the title phrase of this book, *I am My Body,* began to dawn. My hope and prayer is that as you read this book you will have the same experience and come into a new reverence for the dignity of your body and the beauty of your love.

I have many people to thank for the help which I have received in writing this book. First of all I owe a great depth of gratitude to my community here at St Mary's, for their generosity in enabling me to attend several courses on Blessed John Paul's *Theology of the Body* by Christopher West in the USA. His teaching, but most of all his enthusiasm for the truths that John Paul expounded, made a deep impression on me. So too did

---

[1] *Redemptor Hominis* (1979), 10.

the hundreds of men and women who attended those courses. The vast majority of them were married with families. They shared, with joyful enthusiasm, how John Paul's teaching had enriched their family life.

I am grateful to my confrere at St Mary's, Fr Thomas MacCarte, who proofread my manuscript. No misprint or misspelling escaped his detection.

Finally my sincere thanks to Redemptorist Publications for agreeing to bring this book out at the time of the Beatification of Pope John Paul II. It was the announcement of the Beatification that stimulated me to finish the book that I had been writing at a leisurely pace over three years. Despite the short notice the skills of my editors made this publication in time for the Beatification of Pope John Paul II possible.

Fr Jim McManus C.Ss.R.

Chapter One
I am my body

I remember well the excitement I experienced when I first read the words of Pope John Paul in 1981:

> … *what is at issue is not only the body* (understood as an organism in the "somatic" sense) but also the person *who expresses himself or herself by means of that body,* and in this sense, I would say, "is" that body.[1]

In that moment I had a sense that here we have the true vision of what it means to be human, a vision devoid of the dualistic separation of body and soul that plagued theology and spirituality for many centuries. I don't just have a body, *I am my body*. Here was a vision that transcends the tendency to compare, often unfavourably, the body with the soul and to regard the body as of less importance than the soul. This vision of what it means to be human reclaimed the body for both spirituality and theology. It reclaimed the body for the personal and spiritual dimension.

The truth about ourselves contained in that simple expression "I am my body" is more necessary than ever before, because we have a dangerous tendency today to reduce the human body to its biological components. We can indeed reduce the body to "raw material" that can be manipulated in any way science deems fit.[2] If I can say, "I am my body", I am also saying that I am more than the biological make-up of that physical part of me that I call "body". There is something more to being body than having bodily parts. That more is the person.

Blessed John Paul's full statement is:

> It is certainly possible to "describe" the human body, to express its truth with the objectivity proper to the natural sciences; but such a description – with all its precision – cannot be adequate (that is, commensurate with its object), given that *what is at issue is not only the body* (understood as an organism in the "somatic" sense) but also the person *who expresses himself or herself by means of that body…*[3]

---

[1] *Theology of the Body* (Boston: Pauline Press, 2006), 55:2.
[2] *Letter to Families* (1994), 19.
[3] *Theology of the Body,* 55:2.

The body is not just an organism like the body of other living things. The first realisation that Adam had as a person was that his body, although material or physical, was not like the bodies of the animals, although they too were physical and material. Adam couldn't find a helpmate among any of them (Genesis 2:20). What made the human body different was the fact that it manifested the person. Adam broke out into song when he saw Eve: "This one at last is bone of my bones and flesh of my flesh!" (Genesis 2:23). It was as if Adam exclaimed, "look, a body that expresses the person!"[4] Eve was a person, just as he was, and it was her body that manifested her person. The human body, manifesting the person, is imbued with all the dignity and worth of the person. But this dignity of the body was not always defended and proclaimed in theology. Pope Benedict XVI could lament in his first encyclical:

> Nowadays Christianity of the past is often criticized as having been opposed to the body; and it is quite true that tendencies of this sort have always existed. Yet the contemporary way of exalting the body is deceptive. *Eros,* reduced to pure sex has become a commodity, a mere "thing" to be bought and sold, or rather, man himself becomes a commodity.[5]

Pope Benedict draws this sad but inevitable conclusion:

> Here we are actually dealing with a debasement of the human body: no longer is it integrated into our overall existential freedom; no longer is it a vital expression of our whole being, but it is more or less relegated to the purely biological sphere. The apparent exaltation of the body can quickly turn into a hatred of bodiliness.[6]

Notice that the false exaltation of the body can quickly give way to the degradation of the body. Without a true vision of what it means to be a body-person or an embodied spirit it is very difficult to live the dignity of the body. That dignity is undermined by many false maxims such as: "It is only my body," or "I can do what I like with my body." You hear that kind of remark from people who are justifying abortion or selling their bodies for sex. Aids specialist Edward Green, in his recent book, *Broken Promises,* recalls a conversation that a San Francisco health official had with Gaetan Dugas, the man believed to bear more responsibility for spreading Aids in the USA than anyone else. When asked to stop deliberately infecting

---

[4] *Theology of the Body*, 14:5.
[5] *Deus Caritas Est* (2006), 5.
[6] *Deus Caritas Est*, 5.

people, Dugas responded, "It's my right to do what I want to do with my own body."[7] His confused notion of what his body was, was not that different from the view of many people (although in his case it was lethal for many other people): the body is something apart from the person; it is a thing the person uses to get around and do his work; at the end of the day we can say, "It is only my body." Can you imagine someone saying "It is only my person"? We instinctively respect our persons and demand that others do likewise. Why is it, then, that so many people don't seem to have that same respect for their bodies? Blessed John Paul was determined to give a teaching which would enable people to see their bodies in a different light, in a personalistic light, a theological light.

Our core beliefs about ourselves

Christians turn to the Bible, to God's revelation, as the source for their understanding of themselves. Here are just some core beliefs that we hold about ourselves:

- We have been made in the image and likeness of God (Genesis 1).
- We have sinned but have been redeemed (Genesis 3; 2 Corinthians 5:17).
- We are a new creation (2 Corinthians 5:17).
- We are precious in God's sight (Isaiah 43:4).
- We have been made little less than gods and crowned with glory and beauty (Psalm 8:6).
- We are reborn of water and the Holy Spirit (John 3:6).
- Our bodies are the temple of the Holy Spirit (1 Corinthians 6:19).
- We are God's work of art (Ephesians 2:10).
- We are the body of Christ (1 Corinthians 12:27).

Notice how revelation is not just about God revealing himself to us, but about God revealing us to ourselves. Everything God says to us about himself contains a revelation to us about ourselves. If God exists, we are his image; if God dwells anywhere, we are his temple; if God is the divine artist, we are his work of art. That is why the Second Vatican Council said:

> In reality it is only in the mystery of the Word made flesh that the mystery of humanity truly becomes clear. For Adam, the first man, was

---

[7] Edward Green, *Broken Promises: How the Aids Establishment has Betrayed the Developing World* (Sausalito: PoliPoint Press, 2011), 88.

a type of him who was to come, Christ the Lord. Christ the new Adam, in the very revelation of the mystery of the Father and of his love, fully reveals humanity to itself and brings to light its very high calling.[8]

Revelation goes hand in hand with the experience of being human. The experience of being human is a primary source for all theological reflection on what it means to be human. Reflecting on what it means to be human on the basis of abstract principles is not a helpful way of doing theology today. Blessed John Paul was convinced that we can identify the objective truth of what it means to be human by analysing subjective experience. He wrote:

> Our *human experience is in some way a legitimate means for theological interpretation* and… in a certain sense, it is an indispensable point of reference to which we must appeal in the interpretation of the "beginning".[9]

Experience of love

Human experience is the experience of the one who is in the image and likeness of God. We could ask, "How does the image of God on earth experience his or her human life?" What experience teaches us about ourselves is that we cannot live without the experience of love. Indeed in his very first encyclical letter to the Church, Blessed John Paul wrote:

> Humans cannot live without love. They remain beings that are incomprehensible for themselves, their lives are senseless… This is why Christ the Redeemer fully reveals man to himself.[10]

Blessed John Paul's five-year catechetical project

To help us to understand the truth of our own bodies, to understand our need for love, Blessed John Paul undertook a most original catechetical project. Over a five-year period, beginning on 5 September 1979 and concluding on 28 November 1984, he gave 130 general audience addresses on what he called the *Theology of the Body*. He set himself the task of providing an adequate anthropology – that is, the theological way of understanding what it means to be human – for our times. During the course of this five-year magisterial teaching, he cited over a thousand verses of scripture, from forty-six books of the Bible, quoting from 233

---

[8] *Gaudium et Spes* (1965), 22.
[9] *Theology of the Body*, 4:4.
[10] *Redemptor Hominis*, 10.

different chapters. We have had nothing like this kind of Bible-based theological teaching since the time of St Augustine. He gave us, for the first time, a comprehensive theology of the body – a theology of what it means to be human and how the exploration of human experience leads to the knowledge of God. George Weigel, the biographer of Pope John Paul, wrote:

> The Church and the world will be well into the twenty-first century, and perhaps beyond, before Catholic theology has fully assimilated the contents of these 130 general audience addresses. If it is taken with the seriousness that it deserves, John Paul's *Theology of the Body* may prove to be the decisive moment in exorcising the Manichaean demon and its deprecation of human sexuality from Catholic moral theology. Few moral theologians have taken our embodiedness as male and female as seriously as John Paul II… These 130 catechetical addresses, taken together, constitute a kind of theological time bomb set to go off, with dramatic consequences, sometime in the third millennium of the Church.[11]

The spousal meaning of the body

Since we cannot live without love, since life is meaningless without love, we can surely conclude that we are so made, so constituted in our innermost being, that we have both the need for love and the capacity to give love. This capacity for love is constitutive of our very being. We would not be human, we would not be made in the image and likeness of God, without it. Blessed John Paul calls this capacity "the spousal meaning of the body".[12] This is his seminal insight which guides all his exploration of what it means to be human and how to live a life that brings us true happiness. The spousal capacity of the body is, *"the power to express love: precisely that love in which the human person becomes a gift* – and through this gift – *fulfils the very meaning of his or her being and existence"*.[13]

We know we have been made in the image and likeness of God because we have the capacity to love, to make the gift of self to others, just as God, who is love itself, makes the gift of self to us. It is through giving that gift of self, through becoming a gift, that we make a wonderful

---

[11] George Weigel, *Witness to Hope: The Biography of Pope John Paul II* (London: HarperCollins, 1999), 342.
[12] *Theology of the Body*, 31:1.
[13] *Theology of the Body* 15:1.

discovery. The Second Vatican Council said, "Humans can only discover their true selves in sincere self-giving."[14] The spousal capacity of the body enables us to discover our true selves, to discover that we are self-giving. Blessed John Paul says:

> The exchange of gift, in which the whole humanity, soul and body, femininity and masculinity, participates, is realized *by preserving the inner character (that is precisely innocence) of self-donation and of the acceptance of the other as a gift.* These two functions of mutual exchange are deeply connected in the whole process of the "gift of self": giving and accepting the gift interpenetrate in such a way that the very act of giving becomes acceptance, and acceptance transforms itself into giving.[15]

Finding oneself in one's own gift of self

In making the gift of self to the other we discover our true selves. This discovery empowers us to make the gift of self in a new and more authentic way. The dynamic of true love is thus created: becoming a gift to the other and being received by the other as a gift and receiving the other in return as a gift. We find our true selves in our gift. Blessed John Paul elaborates:

> This *finding of oneself in one's own gift becomes the source of a new gift of self* that grows by the power of the inner disposition of the exchange of the gift and in the measure in which it encounters the same and even deeper acceptance and welcome as the fruit of an ever more intense consciousness of the gift itself.[16]

It is the spousal capacity of the body which enables us to image God. This spousal capacity is inscribed in our bodies (not in our minds) by God in the very beginning. We are told, "male and female he created them" (Genesis 1:27). It is in our very masculinity and femininity that God has inscribed his image. Blessed John Paul says:

> The body, which expresses femininity "for" masculinity and vice versa, manifests the reciprocity of the communion of persons. It expresses it through gift as the fundamental characteristic of existence. This is *the body: a witness* to creation as a fundamental

---

[14] *Gaudium et Spes*, 24.
[15] *Theology of the Body*, 14:4.
[16] *Theology of the Body*, 17:5.

gift, and therefore a witness *to Love as the source from which this same giving springs.*[17]

We were created by Love and we were endowed with the capacity to love in return. Our very body, Blessed John Paul says, "is a witness to love". God created men and women with the capacity to love and make the gift of self to one another in marriage, and thus become the source of life and love for their children. Those who are not married can make the sincere gift of self to others in ways appropriate to their state in life. This experience of making the sincere gift of self to the other is what we mean by love: a husband and wife loving one another and giving themselves to each other for life; a Mother Teresa loving the orphans and the dying in Calcutta and giving herself totally to serving them for life; a young man or woman, still hoping for a spouse, and preserving sexual dignity in all their relationships; men and women consecrated to God, living for the service of others. Love is the greatest gift we can offer to another person and the greatest gift we can receive from another. Love is always the gift of self, and, as the Second Vatican Council said, in giving that gift "we discover our true selves".[18] If that gift of self is not being offered, then no matter what else is being offered, it is not love and there will be no discovery of the true self. People know the difference between an act that is fundamentally self-giving and an act that is ultimately self-seeking. We know from experience that a relationship built of true self-giving lasts, while a relationship built on self-seeking will always eventually collapse.

Living out the spousal meaning of the body ensures that the integrity of the other person will always be respected. The gift of self will be made to the other on the level appropriate to the relationship between the giver and the one to whom the gift is given. It will be self-giving not self-seeking. But we know from experience that self-seeking can be a dominating, often almost overwhelming force. We always need the grace of God to live the spousal meaning of the body with joyfulness and integrity. But let us say at the very beginning that this is what God wants for us and indeed this is why Jesus came. As he said, "I have come so that they may have life and have it to the full" (John 10:10). Life to the full, a happy life, a good life, a life that is lived in love and self-giving, that is the gift that Christ wants to give to each of us. And that is what the spousal capacity of the body makes possible for us.

---

[17] *Theology of the Body*, 14:4.
[18] *Gaudium et Spes*, 24.

Not surprisingly, men and women in every age have discussed what it means to love. Indeed Blessed John Paul can say:

> In fact, in the whole perspective of their own "history", men and women will not fail to confer a spousal meaning on their own body. Even if this meaning does undergo and will undergo many distortions, it will always remain the deepest level, which demands that it be revealed in all its simplicity and purity and manifested in its whole truth as a sign of the "image of God". Here we also find the road that goes from the mystery of creation to the "redemption of the body".[19]

We cannot avoid the question of what true love is because love is what gives meaning and purpose to our lives.

The meaning of love does undergo many distortions but we never surrender its true meaning to the distortions. People recognise the real thing when they experience it. Very significantly Pope Benedict wrote his first encyclical to the Church on love, *God is Love*,[20] in which he explores both the mystery of God's love and the nature of human love. And his third encyclical has the title *Caritas in Veritate* ("Love in Truth"). True love can never be divorced from the truth, the truth about God or the truth about us – especially the truth about the meaning of our bodies, through which we love. As Pope Benedict says:

> Without truth charity degenerates into sentimentality. Love becomes an empty shell, to be filled in an arbitrary way. In a culture without truth, this is the fatal risk facing love. It falls prey to contingent subjective emotions and opinions, the word "love" is abused and distorted, to the point where it comes to mean the opposite.[21]

Those who want to love sincerely always want to love in the truth, respecting the truth of their own body and the truth of the one they love. But, as we are well aware, distortions abound. The aim of John Paul's *Theology of the Body* is to provide a new synthesis of theology in which this human need for love, and the experience of love as the fulfilment of human existence, can be discussed, analysed and shared with our generation. It is a theological analysis of what it means to be human and how to be happy. Happiness, as John Paul says, means "being rooted in

---

[19] *Theology of the Body*, 15:5.
[20] *Deus Caritas Est*.
[21] *Caritas in Veritate* (2009), 3.

love".[22] Indeed Pope Benedict sees love as an experience of redemption. He writes in his encyclical on Christian Hope:

> It is not science that redeems man: man is redeemed by love. This applies even in terms of this present world. When someone has the experience of a great love in his life, this is a moment of "redemption" which gives a new meaning to his life.[23]

Human happiness depends on finding true love, while unhappiness is the absence of true love. The fulfilled life is the life enriched by love, the unfulfilled life is the life without love or the life from which true love has been banished. Where does this need for love come from? Why can't the human being be self-sufficient in such a way that there is no need to go outside self and make the gift of self to the other?

The ancient Greek myth of "Androgyne" explained the difference of the sexes as a punishment of the gods. Man was a perfect sexual being, complete in himself, but the gods split him in two, with one half masculine and the other feminine. Since then humans have been searching for their other half.[24] Indeed we often hear a man referring to his wife as his "better half". But the Christian faith has a very different understanding. Both male and female are created equally by God. Each is whole in himself or herself, and each seeks a unity of persons, a communion of persons, as the fullness of life on earth. Both masculinity and femininity are "two incarnations of what it means to be human".[25] God created the sexual difference between man and woman and human fulfilment is achieved, not despite this difference, but because of it. Human fulfilment can only be achieved through love. Sexuality is the power to make the gift of self in love to the other in appropriate ways. It is our sexuality that gives us the capacity to relate.

Transcending self

The Second Vatican Council explained why we are not self-sufficient in this way: "Humans can only discover their true selves in sincere self-giving."[26] If we do not go outside ourselves, transcend ourselves, if we do not make that sincere gift of self, we fail to discover our true selves. Transcending self

---

[22] *Theology of the Body*, 16:2.

[23] *Spe Salvi* (2007), 26.

[24] Pope Benedict refers to this myth in his encyclical, *Deus Caritas Est*, 14.

[25] *Theology of the Body*, 8:1.

[26] *Gaudium et Spes*, 24.

simply means reaching out to others in a way that helps us to grow, to be open to others, to establish communion with others. Failure to transcend self by making the gift of self, causes a deep existential loneliness. The person who refuses to transcend self denies the spousal meaning of the body and fails to discover the beauty of their true self. It is a denial of what John Paul called "the fundamental characteristic of existence" which is to be gift.[27] Many people become isolated and lonely, not because nobody loves them, but because they are refusing to go out in love to anyone. The mutuality of the sincere gift of self requires that we must first make the gift of self to the other before we experience the gift of self that the other makes to us. Or, put more simply, if you want to be loved you must first love. It is the spousal capacity of our bodies which enables us to make the gift of self and thus discover our true selves.

I sum up the truth of my being when I say, "I am my body." And I define what I mean by body with the words of John Paul: "This is *the body: a witness* to creation as a fundamental gift, and therefore a witness *to Love as the source from which this same giving springs.*"[28]

Those who study Blessed John Paul's *Theology of the Body* invariably say, "This is true to my experience", even when his theology calls for a very different way of living. At a conference in the USA on the *Theology of the Body* I heard a young woman say to a hundred young men and women, "I am a Mormon woman and for the first time in my life I have heard the truth about my body, the truth that resonates deep within me." The truth, often so hard to grasp in abstract concepts, has a tendency to hit us in our gut. At the level of the deep heart we understand, we recognise the truth, even if we are not able to articulate cogent arguments to explain or defend it. There is a deep truth in the statement, "I am my body", and as we ponder it we begin to experience it deep within our hearts.

A new way of doing theology

For centuries theology began with abstract, philosophical principles. From those principles theologians deduced further truths of faith. It was an objective and, what is known as, a "deductive" method of doing theology. The principle enshrined the truth. What can be logically deduced from the principle is also true. But in the past three hundred years philosophy has swung from the objective to the subjective. Would theology follow

---

[27] *Theology of the Body*, 14:4.
[28] *Theology of the Body*, 14:4.

suit? There was great fear of the subjective approach. Fifty years ago, when I first began to study theology, I was warned against the dangers of subjectivism. The basic motto was; stick to the principles because they never change. We brought abstract principles to the human condition and interpreted the human condition in the light of the principles. The objective reality came first and the subjective experience had to be interpreted in the light of the objective. Blessed John Paul had a very different methodology. His motto was: don't be afraid of the subjective, don't be afraid of beginning with the subjective, personal experience, because the only way to communicate with the people of our time is to help them discover the truth that is at the heart of their subjective, personal experience. That truth is the truth of their bodies, through which they are having the experience in the first place. That truth of their bodies is the truth of who they are, as the image and likeness of God.

For many centuries we didn't have the theological or philosophical tools to explore human experience in this way. While our faith told us that we were made in the "image and likeness of God" our theology didn't accept that "our human experience is in some way a legitimate means for theological interpretation."[29] The common wisdom was that just as every person's experience is different, so every person's interpretation of experience will be different. We didn't have the theological confidence to say that if God has inscribed in the human being his own image and likeness, then the human being, by sincerely exploring his or her experience of life, will discover the truth of their own being and life. We tended to ask them to first accept the truth of some principles and then interpret their experience in the light of those principles. We were excessively afraid of sheer subjectivism.

Yet, on an abstract level, we were very confident in saying that moral truth is known by reason. The natural law is written in the human heart. We don't need a revelation from God to know the difference between right and wrong. That is made known to us through our conscience. The Second Vatican Council gave us this clear teaching:

> Deep within their consciences men and women discover a law which they have not laid upon themselves and which they must obey. Its voice, ever calling them to love and to do what is good and avoid evil, tells them inwardly at the right moment: do this, shun that. For they have in their hearts a law inscribed by God. Their

---

[29] *Theology of the Body*, 14:4.

dignity rests on observing this law, and by it they will be judged. Conscience is people's most secret core, and their sanctuary. There they are alone with God whose voice echoes in their depths.[30]

Here we have a very clear statement about the interiority of our moral decisions. There is an interior law, an inner voice, a light that shines on our motives. Even if we wanted to, we cannot totally ignore the voice of conscience. It is the voice of our own dignity as the sons and daughters of God. But it is not an infallible voice. At times it can be wrong. As the Vatican Council acknowledged:

> Yet it often happens that conscience goes astray through ignorance which it is unable to avoid, without thereby losing its dignity. This cannot be said of the person who takes little trouble to find out what is true and good, or when conscience is gradually almost blinded through the habit of committing sin.[31]

Because our conscience can be misled at times, by our own confusions over moral issues or indeed by fears, anxieties or worries, we need the light of the Christ, the light of the Gospel, to make true and good decisions in accordance with our human dignity. St Pope Leo the Great said, "Christian, recognise your dignity and, now that you share in God's own nature, do not return to your former base condition by sinning."[32]

The defence of our human dignity requires us to know the truth about ourselves, about how to live the new life that God gives us. We need to walk in the light. Jesus gave the Church the authority to shed that light. He said, "Go, therefore, make disciples of all nations; baptise them in the name of the Father and of the Son and of the Holy Spirit, and teach them to observe all the commands I gave you. And look, I am with you always; yes, to the end of time" (Matthew 28:19-20). In our world, with the clamour of so many different voices and so many different views on what is good and holy, we need the teaching of Christ. As St John says, "The Word was the real light, that gives light to everyone; he was coming into the world" (John 1:9). We are confident that Christ hasn't left us to our own meagre understanding. The Church teaches:

> The human person participates in the light and power of the divine Spirit. By their reason, men and women are capable of understanding

---

[30] *Gaudium et Spes*, 16.

[31] *Gaudium et Spes*, 16.

[32] Cited in *Catechism of the Catholic Church*, 1691.

the order of things established by the Creator. By free will, they are capable of directing themselves toward their true good. They find their perfection in seeking and loving what is true and good.[33]

Our human dignity is preserved both by the voice of our own conscience and the voice of the Church teaching in Christ's name. When the voice of our conscience is not in accord with the voice of the Church we sincerely seek to understand the truth that the Church is teaching. We begin to explore more profoundly our own experience and we allow the light of the Church's teaching to shine on our experience. We hear with new urgency the words of St Paul: "Do not model your behaviour on the contemporary world, but let the renewing of your minds transform you, so that you may discern for yourselves what is the will of God – what is good and acceptable and mature" (Romans 12:2). That teaching of St Paul is as relevant for us today as it was for the first Christians in pagan Rome nearly two thousand years ago. We can conform our minds to the truth of Christ's teaching, or we can allow our minds to be deformed by the confusions and the distortions of the truth which we encounter each day.

Body-soul dualism and a Manichaean tendency

Blessed John Paul was very aware that dualism, with its latent Manichaeanism, is the big heresy about the human person today. We have a glorification of the body, but the body is disconnected from the person. The body is often seen as "the house" in which the person has to live. We can do what we like with our bodies – adorn them, glorify them, use them for our personal pleasure. And we can use the bodies of others in the same way. John Paul wrote in his *Letter to Families*:

> The human family is facing the challenge of a *new Manichaeanism*, in which body and spirit are put in radical opposition; the body does not receive life from the spirit, and the spirit does not give life to the body. Man thus *ceases to live as a person and a subject*. Regardless of all intentions and declarations to the contrary, he becomes merely an *object*.[34]

We cannot divide the human being up into body and soul as if they were separate, independent entities. Without the soul there is no human body and without the human body we would not have a human soul. We are

---

[33] *Catechism of the Catholic Church*, 1704.
[34] *Letter to Families*, 19.

a unity of body and soul. The *Catechism of the Catholic Church* expresses this very clearly:

> The unity of soul and body is so profound that one has to consider the soul to be the "form" of the body: i.e., it is because of its spiritual soul that the body made of matter becomes a living human body: spirit and matter, in humans, are not two natures united, but rather their union forms a single nature.[35]

Body and soul are a unity, a single nature. I don't just have a body, as if that was a separate part of me. Acknowledging the truth expressed in the phrase, *I am my body,* is the first step in gratefully accepting oneself, acknowledging one's true identity. Sadly we meet people who emotionally reject their bodies. They might even tell you that they hate the body they are forced to live in. Rather than seeing the body as the manifestation of the person, they regard it as an obstacle to personal fulfilment. This unhealthy rejection of the body ensures that self-fulfilment will always be elusive, because none of us has any self to fulfil *apart from the embodied self.* Without the body that embodies the self, we wouldn't even exist. Of course, nobody rejects their body without a cause – such as a hurtful remark about someone's looks or shape, or a negative comparison with someone else. It may also be the result of someone's dualistic philosophy – the way they have learned to see themselves. Once people begin to realise that their problem with their bodies is not with the body itself, but with other people's cruel remarks or a false way of viewing their bodies, they begin the process of a healthy self-acceptance and a grateful acceptance of their bodies.

Overcoming dualism

We have to move from a dualistic view that sees the person as separate from the body, to a holistic view that sees the human being as a body-person or an embodied person. John Paul in his *Letter to Families* identified the most recent source of this dualism:

> The philosopher who formulated the principle of "*Cogito ergo sum*", "I think, therefore I am", also gave the modern concept of man its distinctive dualistic character. It is typical of rationalism to make a radical contrast in man between spirit and body. But man is a person in the unity of his body and his spirit. The body can never

---

[35] *Catechism of the Catholic Church,* 365.

be reduced to mere matter: it is a *spiritualised body,* just as man's spirit is so closely united to the body that he can be described as an *embodied spirit.*[36]

The body manifests the person and so each of us can say "I am my body."

Because the body manifests the person, everything the body does manifests what the person is like. And everything done to the body is done to the person. Just as you would allow no one to abuse your person, neither should you allow anyone to abuse your body, because in abusing your body they would be abusing your person. We have, of course, a lot of false thinking lurking around in our culture. Some would say, "It is just your body and you can do what you like with your body." Notice what is going on here. You are being contrasted with your body. It is as if they are saying, "This physical thing that you have that you call your body is not really you, and so you can do whatever you like with it." When we respond that the body reveals the person, and so whatever is done to the body is done to the person, they have to make their dualistic thinking clear. They have to say, the body is really an inferior part of you. It doesn't deserve the same respect that your person does. They are forced to deny the truth that *I am my body.* And now they find it very difficult to explain the relationship between the body and the person.

Just think about how the human body is abused in our society. A very obvious way is in the pornographic industry. A beautiful person's body is exposed, normally in some more or less naked position, and the intent is not to manifest the beauty of the person but to excite lustful feelings in the observer. The image of the body of another person is being used as a means to sexually arouse someone else. But the body can also be used as a weapon to attack another person, or to speak untruths to deceive another person, or to steal, or to rob another person. The body manifests the person and when the person engages in those kinds of activities, then the body manifests a person who is a liar or a cheat or a robber or a pornographer. How often have you heard someone say, after witnessing what someone else has done, "That's not a very nice person." Even if the person is a film star, his or her personality is ultimately judged, not by their looks, but by their behaviour. The body manifests the person. It is what we do and not how we look or try to present ourselves that reveals the kind of person we are. The truth that *I am my body,* that my body manifests my person, underlies the personalistic principle of morality of

---

[36] *Letter to Families,* 19.

Blessed John Paul. Before he became Pope he had published in 1960 his profound study, *Love and Responsibility*, in which he stated his conviction in this way: "Nobody can use a person as a means towards an end, no human being, nor yet God the Creator."[37]

For Blessed John Paul the opposite of *loving* is not *hating*, but *using*. Using another person for one's own advantage or pleasure is always abusing. The personalistic norm in ethics states that the only appropriate response to a person is love. Negatively stated, it holds that a person must never be used as a means to an end, even a good end.

If one loses sight of the dignity of the person as a body-person, or as an *embodied spirit*, and separates the person from the body, one can easily begin using another person's body for one's own advantage, while claiming to respect the person. An erroneous but very ancient and pernicious form of dualism! Science hasn't corrected this dualistic view of human beings. Indeed, one could say that it has magnified it. As Blessed John Paul said:

> Science does not yet develop the consciousness of the body as a sign of the person, as a manifestation of the spirit. The whole development of contemporary science of the body as organism has rather the character of biological knowledge, because it is based on the disjunction between what is bodily and what is spiritual in man.[38]

The whole aim of Blessed John Paul's five-year catechesis on the theology of the body, was to ensure that this disjunction would be banished from theological thinking. And in its place he proposed "a specific spirituality of the body".[39] That will be his great legacy to the Church today.

---

[37] Karol Wojtyla, *Love and Responsibility* (San Francisco: Ignatius Press, 1993), 27.
[38] *Theology of the Body*, 59:3.
[39] *Theology of the Body*, 59:4.

Chapter Two
The body is made in the image of God

There is a deep yearning, one could say an ache in the human heart, that cries out for constant attention. We need to have our yearning satisfied and we need to have our ache alleviated in some way. But very often we don't know what to do. Many of the solutions we've tried, that we were sure would bring the peace that our heart was yearning for, didn't work. The yearning often got worse and the ache became even more intense. Nothing seemed capable of satisfying the needs of the heart. Then one day we discovered, as so many others have, that this yearning and this ache were not problems to be solved, but blessings to be grateful for, because the yearning was for God, and only union with God could alleviate the ache. St Augustine discovered this truth in his search for peace and expressed it this way: "You have made us for yourself, and our hearts find no peace until they rest in you."[1] The yearning and the ache have been implanted in us by God.

A revelation

The surpassing dignity of the human being resides in the fact that humans are created in the image of God. This knowledge has been revealed to us by God. Without the revelation of God we would not know this. We would have known, of course, that human beings are rational, that they can think, love and hate, remember and regret. In these human activities they are unlike animals that act on the level of instinct. We act on the intellectual level, on the spiritual level, on the volitional level. We could say we act on the personal and inter-personal level. But what is it about us human beings that enables us to say that we have been made in the image and likeness of God? Where do we find the image of God in the human being?

When you see a man or woman in the street, what is it about them that is the image of God? What do you see? You see, first of all, the physical body. Is that body the image of God? But, as we reflected in the last chapter, the body manifests the person. Is it the person that is the image

---

[1] *Confessions*, I:1.

of God? In our tradition we speak about "body and soul" – the body being the physical dimension and the soul being the spiritual. So is it the soul that is the image of God? God is pure spirit and therefore doesn't have a body. So we might naturally assume that, if human beings are made in the image of God, it would be the spiritual part that would be so made. The physical or bodily part would not be in the image of God. For over a thousand years of scholastic theology the image of God in men and women was seen as residing solely in the spiritual. St Thomas Aquinas, one of the greatest theologians, wrote, "To be the image of God belongs to the mind only."[2] God is spirit and so, it was presumed, only the spiritual dimension of man could image God. As a boy I was told that my soul was made in the image of God. And many people I speak to today are very surprised when I talk to them about their bodies being made in the image of God. I needed John Paul's *Theology of the Body* before I became convinced of this myself. But the whole Church needs to be convinced of this. We urgently need to pay attention to what he has taught us. John Paul highlighted the bad consequences of this separation:

> The separation of spirit and body in man has led to a growing tendency to consider the human body, not in accordance with the categories of its specific likeness to God, but rather on the basis of its similarity to all other bodies present in the world of nature, bodies which man may use as raw material in his efforts to produce goods for consumption. When the human body... comes to be used as raw material... we will inevitably arrive at a dreadful ethical defeat.[3]

We are living in a time when the human body, cut off from the spiritual dimension, separated from the soul, has been reduced to its biological and physical components. The body has been reduced to the status of an object that can be used and manipulated or exploited by others, or even by oneself. John Paul calls this reduction of the body the "new Manichaeanism":

> The human family is facing the challenge of a *new Manichaeanism*, in which the body and spirit are put in radical opposition... Men and women thus cease to live as persons and subjects. Regardless of all intentions and declarations to the contrary, they become objects. This neo-Manichaean culture has led, for example, to

---

[2] *Summa Theologiae*, I, q.93, a.6.
[3] *Letter to Families*, 19.

human sexuality being regarded more as an area for manipulation and exploitation than as a basis for that primordial wonder which led Adam on the morning of creation to exclaim before Eve: This at last is bone of my bones and flesh of my flesh.[4]

As we saw in the last chapter, it is the body that manifests the person. We don't have a body, we are our body. Your body is the visible manifestation of your person and it should never be reduced to the status of an object. In the reduction of the body to the status of an object, John Paul sees one of the great heresies of our time – the re-emergence of the very old heresy of Manichaeanism.

Rationalism

Rationalism, a system of thought which denies the mystery of God and therefore the mystery of human beings, cannot tolerate mystery. It is totally agreeable, then, to rationalism to separate the human being into body and soul, and lay claim to the body that it can touch and feel and manipulate according to its own lights. And in the rationalistic perspective there is nothing sacred about the human body. The body is reduced to its biological or chemical components. The human, physical body, of course, is composed of these components but that is no reason for concluding that there is nothing else to the human body except these components. There is much more. There is humanness. As John Paul said:

> The body reveals the person. This concise formula already contains all that human science will ever be able to say about the structure of the body as an organism.[5]

Everything that makes the human being resides in the body.

The human body is never a thing apart from the human person or the human spirit. The body is always an embodied spirit. As an embodied spirit the human being has imprinted on his or her bodily existence the capacity to love and receive love, the ability to make a true gift of self in an appropriate way. As we saw in the last chapter John Paul called this capacity "the spousal meaning of the body", and defined it as: "*the power to express love: precisely that love in which the human person becomes a*

---

[4] *Letter to Families*, 19.
[5] *Theology of the Body*, 9:4.

gift – and through this gift – fulfils the very meaning of his or her being and existence."[6]

The body has imprinted on it the creative and beatifying word, "self-donation". Living self-donation to the full leads to deep, inner peace and fulfilment; living self-gratification to the full leads to a disintegration of self. The capacity to love, to make that sincere gift of self, enables man and woman to become a communion of persons – the image of God, who is a communion of persons – Father, Son and Holy Spirit. In seeking to live in communion we are living out the image of God, actualising our most human potential.

The body is in the image of God

John Paul had no hesitation in teaching that the body too is made in the image of God. You cannot in fact separate body and soul and think of either of them apart. The human person is only a person because the body is informed by the soul, or because the soul informs the body. The body is human because of the soul and likewise the soul is human because of the body. The Catholic Church teaches today that "spirit and matter, in humans, are not two natures united, but rather their union forms a single nature."[7] As John Paul said: "The body can never be reduced to mere matter: it is a *spiritualised body,* just as man's spirit is so closely united to the body that he can be described as an *embodied spirit.*"[8]

God is self-giving love

But we can ask the question, how can the body image God? What enables the body to image God? God is a pure spirit and invisible. How could the visible human body image the invisible God? And what is it that we are imaging when we are imaging God? We are not imaging his infinite power but his unconditional love. As St John said, "God is love" (1 John 4:8). Love is self-giving. Whatever images God has to be capable of imaging love as self-giving, capable of making the gift of self. Because the body has this power to express love, to make the gift of self to the other in love, the body can image God, who is love. Indeed, as John Paul said: "In the mystery of creation, the human body carried within itself an unquestionable sign of the image of God."[9]

---

[6] *Theology of the Body,* 15:1.
[7] *Catechism of the Catholic Church,* 365.
[8] *Letter to Families,* 19.
[9] *Theology of the Body,* 27:3.

Since all human love is expressed through the body, the body has the best of all capacity for imaging God. John Paul expresses this very strongly when he said:

> The body, in fact, and only the body, is capable of making visible what is invisible: the spiritual and the divine. It was created to transfer into the visible reality of the world the mystery hidden from eternity in God, and thus to be a sign of it.[10]

Finding our true self in sincere self-giving

This capacity that the body has for expressing love, making visible what is invisible, enables the person to make the gift of self to the other. It is only through our body, through our bodily presence with and for others, that we can love. And it is only in this relationship of loving presence with others that we can find our true selves. As the Vatican Council said, men and women "can only find their true selves through sincere self giving."[11] We don't find ourselves in self-seeking. Selfishness is not the road to self-discovery, because selfishness cannot image God. When we give ourselves in love, we activate the image of God within ourselves, and in this way we discover our true selves. The true self, made in the image of God, is the self-giving self, not the self-seeking self. Self-giving is another name for true love. We find our true self in love which is always self-giving and never self-seeking.

Human happiness is the fruit of self-giving love. As John Paul said, "happiness is being rooted in love."[12] God created us in his own image and likeness, created us to be happy, and he endowed our very bodies with the capacity that alone can make us happy, namely the capacity to make the sincere gift of our self to the other and thus fulfil the meaning of our existence. In making that sincere gift of self we realise in whose image we are made and we enter into the mystery of God's self-giving love. Self-giving love is always a participation in God's love. We see the image of God in the human body precisely in this capacity for making that sincere gift of self in love, in this spousal capacity of the body. But we are also aware, through our own experience, that making that sincere gift of self in self-giving love demands great self-discipline and self control on our part. In Chapter four we will consider why doing the very thing

---

[10] *Theology of the Body*, 19:4.
[11] *Constitution on the Church in the Modern World*, 22.
[12] *Theology of the Body*, 16:2.

that enables us to discover our true selves, namely making the sincere gift of self, should be so challenging for us.

The communion of persons images God

John Paul said:

> *Man became the image of God not only through his own humanity, but also through the communion of persons,* which man and woman form from the very beginning. The function of image is that of mirroring the one who is the model, of reproducing the prototype. Man becomes the image of God not so much in the moment of solitude as in the moment of communion. He is, in fact, "from the beginning" not only an image in which the solitude of one Person, who rules the world, mirrors itself, but also and essentially the image of an inscrutable divine communion of Persons.[13]

God has revealed his innermost being to us as a divine communion of Father, Son and Holy Spirit. The image of God in us, therefore, must reflect this communion. We were not created to live as isolated individuals. We were created to live in a communion of persons, in a communion of love, that reflects the communion of Father, Son and Holy Spirit. That is why we read those words in the story of our creation, "It is not right that the man should be alone. I shall make him a helper" (Genesis 2:18). Alone, in his isolated solitude, Adam could not image the triune God. He could not fulfil the meaning of his existence which is to live in love and so he could not experience happiness. In the story of creation we are told that God brought all the animals to Adam but he couldn't find one like himself among any of them. God then put Adam into a deep sleep and took one of his ribs and created Eve. When he brought Eve to Adam we heard the first love song of history. Adam exclaimed, "This one at last is bone of my bones and flesh of my flesh!" (Genesis 2:23). Carl Anderson comments:

> The book of Genesis uses the Hebrew word *kenegdo* to refer to Eve's identity as a helpmate who is similar to, and on par with, Adam. Literally, *kenegdo* means "to stand face-to-face with another". Adam and Eve look each other in the eye. Identical in humanity, yet different in their respective embodied expressions of humanity.[14]

---

[13] *Theology of the Body*, 9:3.
[14] Carl Anderson and Jose Granados, *Called to Love* (New York: Doubleday, 2009), 47.

John Paul wrote, "Adam simply affirms the human identity of both. By exclaiming this he seems to say, 'Look, a body that expresses the 'person'!'"[15] Adam is recognising in Eve a person like himself. His solitude in a world of animals has been broken because now he can share his life, realise the spousal meaning of his body, enter into a communion of persons with Eve. The story of creation concludes with the words, "This is why a man leaves his father and mother and becomes attached to his wife, and they become one flesh" (Genesis 2:24). The story of the creation is not complete until we are told about the union of Adam and Eve in marriage. Now we have the human communion of persons mirroring the divine communion of persons.

The meaning of original nakedness

The Bible gives us a further insight into the communion of persons which Adam and Eve formed: "Now, both of them were naked, the man and his wife, but they felt no shame before each other" (Genesis 2:25). Why does the Bible include this detail? John Paul responds that original nakedness, "... *in the first biblical sketch of anthropology is not something accidental. On the contrary, it is precisely the key for understanding it fully and completely.*"[16] How can nakedness without shame be a key for understanding humanity as God intended it to be?

As the story unfolds we begin to see the true significance of that original nakedness. God told Adam that he could eat the fruit of all the trees in the garden except the tree of knowledge of good and evil. God said that the day he would eat of that tree he would die (Genesis 2:17). Despite this divine warning of the lethal nature of the fruit on that tree, our first parents, in the moment of being tempted by the serpent, ate the fruit. A bad choice! The consequences happened. The Bible simply states, "Then the eyes of both of them were opened and they realised that they were naked" (Genesis 3:7).

Before they ate of the tree, they were naked without shame; after they ate, their eyes were opened and they experienced shame. John Paul sees shame as a "boundary experience"[17] between the state of original innocence and the state of human sinfulness. Being naked without shame reveals the quality of Adam and Eve's subjective feelings. The lack

---

[15] *Theology of the Body*, 14:4.
[16] *Theology of the Body*, 11:2.
[17] *Theology of the Body*, 11:3.

of shame was not due to blindness, but to their mutual understanding of the spousal meaning of their bodies. They were gifts to one another. It was because of how they saw and understood the truth of their bodies that they felt no shame. Shame enters when their understanding of the meaning of their bodies changes. This is the boundary between original innocence and historical sinfulness. What are they ashamed of? We are told, "They sewed fig-leaves together to make themselves loin-cloths" (Genesis 3:7). They were ashamed of their sexuality and covered the bodily signs of their masculinity and femininity. In that experience of their eyes being opened something changed in the way they understood the meaning of their bodies. Their mutual experience of their bodies changed. God said to Adam, "Who told you that you were naked? Have you been eating from the tree I forbade you to eat?" (Genesis 3:11). They had begun to see themselves in a new way. It was as if somebody had pointed something out to them. John Paul writes:

> It is not a question of passing from "not knowing" to "knowing", but of *a radical change in the meaning of the original nakedness* of the woman before the man and of the man before the woman. This change emerges from their consciousness as a fruit of the tree of knowledge of good and evil. This change directly concerns the experience of the meaning of one's own body before the Creator and creatures.[18]

Being without shame was the result of seeing each other in the mystery of creation, "with the peace of the interior gaze,"[19] because in the mystery of creation, God said "It was very good" (Genesis 1:31). Everything that God had made, everything about Adam and Eve, was very good. Adam and Eve shared in that vision of the goodness of all creation. They saw their bodies as very good, reflecting the glory of God. They were the image of God in the world. After their sin, Adam and Eve no longer shared in this divine vision and saw their nudity as a cause for shame. They had lost the sense of the goodness of their bodies. We traditionally say they had *fallen from grace*. They were no longer seeing one another in the grace of God. John Paul explains:

> With the entrance of shame, it is as if he experienced that he had simply ceased, also through his body and his sex, to remain above the world of living beings or *animalia*. It is as if he had experienced a

---

[18] *Theology of the Body*, 11:5.
[19] *Theology of the Body*, 13:1.

specific *fracture of the personal integrity of his own body, particularly in that which determines its sexuality* and which is directly linked with the call to that unity in which man and woman "become one flesh." (Genesis 2:24)[20]

Indeed, as he writes elsewhere, "Man in some way loses the original certainty of the image of God expressed in his body."[21] Man and woman have become unsure of their greatest dignity. They are no longer in a peaceful acceptance of themselves, of their body-selves. Their nakedness has disturbed their inner peace. John Paul explored with great depth and precision why this should be so. He writes:

> Only the nakedness that turns the woman into an "object" for man, or vice versa, is a source of shame. The fact that "they did not feel shame" means that the woman was not an "object" for the man nor he for her… Inner innocence as "purity of heart" made it impossible somehow for the one to be reduced by the other to the level of a mere object. If "they did not feel shame", this means that they were united by the consciousness of the gift, that they had *reciprocal awareness of the spousal meaning of their bodies,* in which the freedom is expressed and *the whole inner richness of the person as subject is shown.*[22]

Their experience of their bodies has changed. More precisely we can say their experience of the spousal meaning of their bodies has changed. Their bodies, made in the image of God, made to be the medium of self-giving, have become, in some measure, the medium of self-seeking. That is precisely what they are ashamed of. Something new, something alien to the goodness of creation, has begun to motivate their relationship.

Concupiscence

Adam and Eve no longer accept themselves as God has made them. And their shame is not a negative response. In fact, their shame now provides a positive role. What they are ashamed of is not the naked body but, as John Paul said, "the body motivated by concupiscence."[23] This is the new reality in their experience of one another. Concupiscence, or lust, which we will consider in detail in Chapter four, is the opposite of the desire

---

[20] *Theology of the Body,* 28:4.
[21] *Theology of the Body,* 27:3.
[22] *Theology of the Body,* 19:2.
[23] *Theology of the Body,* 28:5.

to make a gift of self. It is an urge to depersonalise and use the other, and take possession of the other as an object for oneself. It was because of this new reality in their experience of one another that they were ashamed. And so, we are told in the Bible, "they hid" (Genesis 3:8). They were aware that they had lost their original innocence, lost the interior grace and freedom of seeing and accepting one another as God created them. John Paul can say:

> One can even say that, through shame, man and woman almost remain in the state of original innocence. In fact, they continually become conscious of the spousal meaning of the body and intend to protect it, so to speak, from concupiscence, just as they try to maintain the value of communion or union of persons in the unity of the body.[24]

After original sin, man and woman lost the grace of original innocence, that gift which enabled them to see each other as gifts from God and see the spousal meaning of their bodies as the capacity for making the sincere gift of self to one another. But God did not leave them without grace. The image of God was still inscribed in the body, imprinted on the spousal meaning of the body, but as John Paul explains at length:

> … the discovery of the spousal meaning of the body was to cease being for them a simple reality of revelation and of grace. Yet, this meaning was to *remain as a task given to man by the ethos of the gift*, inscribed in the depth of the human heart as a distant echo, as it were, of original innocence. From that spousal meaning, human love was to be formed in its interior truth and authentic subjectivity. And even through the veil of shame, man was continually to discover himself in it as the guardian of the mystery of the subject, that is, of the freedom of the gift, in order to defend this freedom from any reduction to the position of a mere object.[25]

The body, even the body motivated by concupiscence or lust, hasn't ceased to be the image of God. The deepest yearning in the human heart is to be united with the God in whose image we are made. Consequently, we seek to protect that image from defilement. That is the positive role of shame. To feel shamed at being treated as an object by others, or to feel shame at treating others as objects, is the right way to feel. We don't

---

[24] *Theology of the Body*, 31:1.
[25] *Theology of the Body*, 19:2.

try to free ourselves from that positive shame. It is, in fact, a reminder to us that our bodies are made in the image of God and that we should reverence them. That is why we can say that the first step in a true spirituality is to accept our body as God's gift. St Paul says:

> Do you not realise that your body is the temple of the Holy Spirit, who is in you and whom you received from God? You are not your own property, then; you have been bought at a price. So use your body for the glory of God. (1 Corinthians 6:19-20)

St Paul also says, "I urge you, then, brothers, remembering the mercies of God, to offer your bodies as a living sacrifice, dedicated and acceptable to God" (Romans 12:1). St Paul held the human body in the highest esteem. He believed in and experienced the redemption of the body (Romans 8:23). We too should cultivate a good esteem of our bodies because, to esteem our bodies is to have healthy self-esteem and give glory to God in whose image our bodies are made.

Sincere self-giving in relationships holds the key to personal growth and development because without it we cannot discover our true selves. Doing something for love, not for gain, even though great gain may be the fruit of it, is the only way to develop personal relationships. A business relationship is for gain; a personal relationship is for the love of the other person and should always bear the hallmark of sincere self-giving. Then, and only then, can the true self be discovered and exchanged. The enrichment of both in the relationship comes from mutual self-giving. This mutuality creates the dynamic, not only of self-giving, but of the concomitant self-discovery which is the fruit of the sincere self-giving. And, can you imagine the quality and the graciousness of the *communion of persons* which is established, fostered and developed by the daily sincere gift of self? That is the image of God. As John Paul said: "*Man became the image of God not only through his own humanity, but also through the communion of persons,* which man and woman form from the very beginning."[26]

That *communion of persons* is now possible because of the spousal capacity of the body. Thus, if we have to answer the question, "What is it about the human body that is in the image of God?" we can say it is the capacity to love by making the sincere gift of self and thus we can say that the image of God in the body resides in the spousal capacity of the body.

---

[26] *Theology of the Body*, 9:3.

Chapter Three
The body is a sacrament: a sign

When we say that we have been created in the image and likeness of God we are saying two things at once. We are saying that the human being, in his or her body, not only images God, but that the body has the capacity to point to the divine. We are saying that in some way the body is a sacrament. Our traditional definition of sacrament is that it is: *"an outward sign of inward grace"*. We could say that the sacrament is the visibility of the invisible. Grace is invisible, but the outward sign of the sacrament, which we can see and touch, manifests and points to the grace. So, for instance, baptism is a sacrament, but the grace of baptism is not visible. The pouring of the water is visible and the words, "I baptise you in the name of the Father and of the Son and of the Holy Spirit" are audible. The invisible of the grace is known through the visible of the sacrament. Christ, we believe, died for his bride the Church and unites himself to his bride. St Paul tells us that "the one flesh union of husband and wife" is the sign of that union. Marriage is a sacrament. The visible union of husband and wife is the sacramental sign of the invisible grace of marriage.

The human body is a sign, a symbol that points to something beyond. John Paul put it this way:

> The sacrament, as a visible sign, is constituted with man, inasmuch as he is a "body", through his "visible" masculinity and femininity. The body, in fact, and only the body, is capable of making visible what is invisible: the spiritual and the divine.[1]

The body is a theology

The body is not simply a biology; the body is a theology; it is a sacramental reality. The human body is the primordial manifestation of God in the world. John Paul says:

> In man, created in the image of God, the very Sacramentality of creation, the Sacramentality of the world, was in some way revealed. In fact, through his bodiliness, his masculinity and femininity, man becomes a visible sign of the economy of Truth and Love, which has

---

[1] *Theology of the Body*, 19:4.

its source in God himself and was revealed already in the mystery of creation.[2]

As a sign or symbol of the divine, what we do with our bodies points to something beyond our bodies, to the life of God that transcends our bodies. If there was nothing more to me than my own physical body, then I could do what I like with it. But there is something more. What I do with my body reflects beyond me, to something greater and altogether more holy than me. And this revelatory capacity of my body doesn't depend on my own will. It is there whether I will it or not. That is what we mean by speaking of the sacramentality of the body or the body as a sacrament. By the very fact that the body has been created in the image and likeness of God it can never lose this sacramental character. It will always point to something beyond. Blessed John Paul writes:

> Man appears in the visible world as the highest expression of the divine gift, because he bears within himself the inner dimension of the gift. And with it he carries into the world his particular likeness to God... Thus in this dimension, a primordial *sacrament* is constituted, understood as a *sign that* efficaciously *transmits in the visible world the invisible mystery hidden in God from eternity.*[3]

God has inscribed in our very being, in our masculinity and our femininity, the capacity to reveal the inner nature of God. "Male and female he created them" (Genesis 1:27). The sexual difference is, according to Christian faith, God's design for the happiness, the fulfilment and the procreation of the human race. It is not an accidental difference. It constitutes human identity. Throughout history humans have identified themselves by reference to their gender – male or female. We cannot separate sex and gender, reducing sex to the purely biological and gender to the purely cultural. Human sex is both biological and personal. Indeed we say it is theological because it is through sexual difference that we image God. We can see the corrosive effect of modern theories that gender is simply a cultural construct. For instance:

> At the United Nations Habitat Conference held in Istanbul in 1996 some theorists argued strongly for five "genders" comprised of heterosexual men and heterosexual women, homosexual men and homosexual women, and transsexuals. While this view was

---

[2] *Theology of the Body*, 19:5.
[3] *Theology of the Body*, 19:3-4.

not adopted by the conference, it continues to be debated in the United Nations and elsewhere both as theory and social policy.[4]

The gift of God, inscribed in our sexuality, has the capacity to reveal God. Thus, St Paul can say that the flesh union of husband and wife reveals the union of Christ and the Church (Ephesians 5:21-32). The body "efficaciously transmits in the visible world the invisible mystery hidden in God from eternity."[5] What is this mystery? The Catechism answers this way:

> God's very being is love. By sending his only Son and the Spirit of Love in the fullness of time, God has revealed his innermost secret. God himself is an eternal exchange of love, Father, Son and Holy Spirit, and he has destined us to share in that exchange.[6]

Our bodies have the capacity to adumbrate or make visible the inner nature of God. This dimension of the human body is the sacramental dimension. You may ask, "But how could our bodies do that?" Most people have never looked at their bodies in this way and find it very hard to accept. We can only answer by repeating that God made our bodies in his own image and likeness. Unpacking what we mean by that phrase takes time, prayer, contemplation and patience. Can my body, my physical being in this world, make visible the invisible God? I may be more aware of its weaknesses than its sacramentality. I may be more conscious of its vulnerability than its capacity for "transmitting into the visible world the mystery hidden in God from eternity."[7] And yet this is the good news, the gospel of the human body as image of God.

All our emotions

The body with all its emotions, feelings and senses, makes visible what is invisible. God's love is invisible, yet becomes visible when I encounter a loving person. And my encounter with that loving person takes place through my body with all its senses and emotions. The principle of knowledge is that there is nothing in the intellect that was not first in the senses. I come to know through my senses. When I meet someone, it is through my senses that I become aware of the person. The impression the

---

[4] John S. Grabowski, *Sex and Virtue: An Introduction to Sexual Ethics* (Washington DC: Catholic University of America Press, 2003), 97.
[5] *Theology of the Body*, 19:4.
[6] *Catechism of the Catholic Church*, 221.
[7] *Catechism of the Catholic Church*, 221.

person makes on me is registered first in my senses, feelings, emotions, attraction or aversion. Before he became Pope, John Paul studied in depth the role that emotions play in living the life of love. Such was his enthusiasm and admiration for the gift and miracle of love, that he devoted years of study to it. And, contrary to what some commentators have said, he plumbed the emotional depths of love. The man who gave the Church the *Theology of the Body* didn't spiritualise love but found love where it belongs, namely in the body, the heart, the emotions, and in the struggles and failures of human beings. In his first letter to the Church he proclaimed the truth that he pondered for so long: "Humans cannot live without love."[8] Since love is so integral to the experience of being human, it is essential for human happiness that it is not confused with counterfeits. Because of the presence of concupiscence or lust in the human heart (which is considered in the next chapter) we know we have to purify our love. True love develops through integrity, honesty and sincere self-giving. For that quality of love we always need purification.

When we want to offer the beautiful gift of love to another person, self-mastery, or purification of our motives, is the means by which we protect that gift from the lusts that can lie hidden in our own hearts. The heart, because of our sinfulness, has become, as John Paul said, "a battlefield".[9] We have to fight for the integrity of our love. But the battle for true love is well worth fighting for because, as Pope Benedict says:

> Love is indeed "ecstasy", not in the sense of a moment of intoxication, but rather as a journey, an ongoing exodus out of the closed inward-looking self towards its liberation through self-giving, and thus towards authentic self-discovery and indeed the discovery of God.[10]

This is the journey of a lifetime. Whenever we lose our way, through our own confusions or weaknesses, we have the compass of self-discovery to hand, which enables us to follow the path of self-giving again, and rediscover our true selves.

St Augustine said that the emotions are the "feet of the soul, by which we either walk toward God or away from him."[11] But turning towards

---

[8] *Redemptor Hominis*, 10.
[9] *Theology of the Body*, 32:3.
[10] *Deus Caritas Est*, 6.
[11] Cit. Carl Anderson and Jose Grandados, *Called to Love* (New York: Doubleday, 2009), 58.

God should never imply turning away from people. Rather, as we turn in love towards people we find the presence of God among them. Love is at once physical and spiritual, emotional and intellectual. Love gives meaning to our existence and becomes the very reflection of God within us. Through love the body shines as a sacrament or sign of the invisible reality of God's grace and presence.

The attractions of the heart, emotions and feelings are all properties of the body, and all point to something more, something outside the body. None of them can achieve satisfaction except in the context of seeking the goal towards which they point – namely, fulfilling the *spousal meaning of the body*, making the sincere gift of self. The goal of all our well-ordered emotions is the *communion of persons*. These emotions have to be integrated into the whole expression of human love. We can only love in and through all our emotions, providing they have been integrated into the process of making the sincere gift of self. People, for instance, who seek to satisfy their yearning for sexual pleasure outside the context of the total gift of self to the beloved, discover over time, that the very pleasure they sought begins to wane and the very person they loved because they satisfied them sexually is no longer desirable. However, as Carl Anderson points out:

> Reducing love to feelings alone isolates us in a prison of egoism, yet leaving feelings out of account is almost as bad, for according to Pope John Paul it deprives our love of warmth and undermines our capacity for real union with another person.[12]

No moral theologian in the 1950s or 1960s gave more attention to the essential role of emotions in preparing for the true manifestation of love, that authentic gift of self, than John Paul when he was Professor of Ethics in Poland. As a student of moral theology in those decades, I was amazed when, many years later, I discovered *Love and Responsibility* which Karol Wojtyla published in 1959. Writing about the need for the emotion of sympathy in the development of love and friendship he said:

> Friendship consists in a full commitment of the will to another person with a view to that person's good. There is, therefore, a need for sympathy to ripen into friendship and this process normally demands time and reflection. While it remains within the limits of sympathy, the attitude to the other person and to his or her value

---

[12] Anderson and Grandados, *Called to Love*, 56.

rests on emotion: what is necessary is to supplement the value of that emotion with an objective knowledge of and belief in the value of the person... On the other hand, it is also necessary to supplement friendship with sympathy, without which it will remain cold and incommunicable. This process is possible, for although sympathy is born in human beings spontaneously and persists irrationally, it gravitates in the direction of friendship, it has a tendency to become friendship. This is a direct consequence of the structure of the inner self of the person, in which only things fully justified by free will and belief acquire full value.[13]

The personalistic norm

The emotions are signs that the body finds fulfilment outside itself, not turned in on itself, but towards the other. The emotions point us to our need for relationships, for that *communion of persons* which truly images God. In all our relationships we experience God-given emotions and these should lead us, not only to others – in friendship, loving collaboration, peaceful co-existence – but also to God. How do I see others with whom I work or towards whom I feel attracted? Do I see them as persons, unique in themselves, existing in their own right, or as somehow existing for my pleasure, my purposes or advantage? In the Bible we are given the basis for proper relationship with each person: "Love your neighbour as yourself" (Matthew 22:39). Jesus was even more specific as to the extent of this love: "But I say this to you, love your enemies and pray for those who persecute you" (Matthew 5:44). The *feel* of the love, or *the emotion* of the love for friend and enemy will, of course, be very different. The emotion of a man's love for his wife will be very different from his love for his friends. But love, not emotion, determines the quality and rightness of the relationship with friend and foe alike. If there is anything lacking in my love for the other, then the relationship is not right. And how do I discern the quality of my love? As a professor in Poland, John Paul laid down this principle in ethics:

> Whenever a person is the object of your activity, remember that you may not treat that person as only the means to an end, as an instrument, but must allow for the fact that he or she, too, has, or at least should have, distinct personal ends. This principle, thus

---

[13] *Love and Responsibility*, 92.

formulated, lies at the basis of all the human freedom, properly understood and especially freedom of conscience.[14]

He called this "the personalistic norm" and defined it in this way: "A person is an entity of a sort to which the only proper and adequate way to relate is love." The opposite of the personalistic norm is the utilitarian norm. John Paul defined it in this way: "The utilitarian norm points to pleasure not only as the basis on which we act but as the basis for rules of human behaviour."[15] In a relationship I am either respecting the unique dignity of the other person, wishing his or her good, or I am using the other person as a means for my own good or satisfaction. Using people is the opposite of loving them. Using people, even for a good purpose, is always immoral. Indeed Karol Wojtyla could write:

> Nobody can use a person as a means to an end, no human being, nor yet God the creator. On the part of God, indeed, it is totally out of the question, since, by giving men and women an intelligent and free nature, he has thereby ordained that each person alone will decide for himself or herself the ends of their activity and not be a blind tool of someone else's end.[16]

Love is a whole body experience. It is both physical and spiritual, emotional and intellectual. Love is the most personal activity we can engage in because in love we are making the sincere gift of ourselves to the other in an appropriate way. As Pope Benedict wrote:

> It is neither the spirit alone nor the body alone that loves: it is man, the person, a unified creature composed of body and soul, who loves. Only when both dimensions are truly united, does man attain his full stature. Only thus is love – eros – able to mature and attain its authentic grandeur.[17]

Sadly, as we know, the meaning of the word *erotic* is restricted to those things that excite sexual and more often lustful feelings. It has lost its sacramental meaning of "making visible what is invisible: the spiritual and divine."[18] Yet, in its original meaning, *eros*, "signifies the inner power

---

[14] *Love and Responsibility*, 28.
[15] *Love and Responsibility*, 40.
[16] *Love and Responsibility*, 27.
[17] *Deus Caritas Est*, 5.
[18] *Theology of the Body*, 19:4.

that attracts humans to the true, the good, and the beautiful."[19] But when erotic means lustful, it loses its original meaning and beauty.

True erotic love empowers the lover to want to make the true gift of self to the beloved. Erotic love, with its strong feelings, yearns for the "true, the good and the beautiful" in the beloved. That is what excites the erotic love in the lover. Here we see the real distinction between love and lust. The power of lust can distort this desire to make the sincere gift of self and turn the yearning for "the true, the good and the beautiful" into a demand for self-satisfaction through the other. As Pope Benedict said:

> *Eros,* reduced to pure "sex", has become a commodity, a mere "thing" to be bought and sold, or rather, man himself becomes a commodity. This is hardly man's great "yes" to the body. On the contrary, he now considers his body and his sexuality as the purely material part of himself, to be used and exploited at will.[20]

Men and women can lose sight of the dignity of their bodies, of the glory of God reflected in their bodies, and they can ignore the truth that they "can only discover their true selves in sincere self-giving."[21] Men and women know through their own experience that if, in their loving, they are seeking "the true, the good and the beautiful", the way of true love will always be one of purification. As Pope Benedict says:

> Love now becomes concern and care for the other. No longer is it self-seeking, a sinking in the intoxication of happiness; instead it seeks the good of the beloved; it becomes renunciation and it is ready, and even willing, for sacrifice.[22]

In love we want to put the good of the other person first; we want to make the sincere gift of self in the appropriate way; we always act according to the personalistic norm and never act according to the utilitarian norm. The person motivated only by self-seeking love, always seeking gratification in love, has never experienced the power of true love nor the dignity of his or her own body.

The dignity, we could say the nobility, of the human body is sacramental because it is the visible sign of God's gift. God didn't have to create human beings. His decision to create was entirely free and gratuitous.

---

[19] *Theology of the Body,* 47:5.
[20] *Deus Caritas Est,* 5.
[21] *Gaudium et Spes,* 24.
[22] *Deus Caritas Est,* 6.

God didn't have to pour out his love on human beings. As St John said, "he first loved us" (1 John 4:19). The human body is the sign or the sacrament of that love. As John Paul said:

> Gift, being gift, is the fundamental characteristic of personal existence. This is *the body: a witness* to creation as a fundamental gift, and therefore a witness *to Love as the source from which this same giving springs.*[23]

The human body is the sign or sacrament of the love of God which is the source and cause of our very existence. The body is the "witness" to God's creative love and, as such, points towards God. Indeed, as we have seen, John Paul's whole thesis is that, in all our relationships, we are capable, through our bodies, of making the spiritual and divine visible.[24] What a profound change of behaviour takes place when men and women wake up to the dignity of their bodies!

Accepting our bodies, then, involves accepting this sacramental dimension. Our bodies, despite all our weaknesses, point us and others towards God. The body always speaks the fundamental truth of its existence, namely, that God has created human beings as male and female. Our sexuality is not of secondary significance in God's plan of creation. It is through our sexuality that God identifies how he is creating us: "male and female he created them" (Genesis 1:27). Our sexuality enters into our very understanding of the body as a sacramental sign of the image of God. John Paul said:

> The sacrament, as a visible sign, is constituted with man, in as much as he is "a body", through his visible masculinity and femininity… In man, created in the image of God, the very sacramentality of creation, the sacramentality of the world, was thus in some way revealed. In fact, through his bodiliness, his masculinity, and femininity, man becomes a visible sign of the economy of Truth and Love, which has its source in God himself and was revealed already in the mystery of creation.[25]

---

[23] *Theology of the Body*, 14:4.
[24] *Theology of the Body*, 19:4.
[25] *Theology of the Body*, 19:5.

The language of the body

Our bodies, created by love and for love, speak what John Paul called "the language of the body".[26] Our sexuality is intrinsic to who we are as human beings. It is in our sexuality that God has inscribed the spousal meaning of the body. The body speaks its truth through its spousal meaning.

Accurately reading this non-verbal language, and refusing to be deceived by the many distorting images from our culture, is the way to integration and inner peace. Who can tell us the truth of our bodies? Our sex-obsessed society, or teachers of the Christian faith, such as John Paul II? The Second Vatican Council said:

> In reality it is only in the mystery of the Word made flesh that the mystery of humanity truly becomes clear. For Adam, the first man, was a type of him who was to come, Christ the Lord. Christ the new Adam, in the very revelation of the mystery of the Father and of his love, fully reveals humanity to itself and brings to light its very high calling.[27]

The truth about ourselves and about the sacramental dignity of our bodies, is revealed by Christ. The challenge to our generations is this: will we listen to Christ's word about the dignity of our bodies created "in the image of God", or will we accept the prevailing sexualised understanding of the human body? Our modern culture wants to depersonalise and de-sacramentalise the body. The result is that the body simply becomes an object for use. It is so sad to see people, infatuated with one another, believing that they are truly in love, divorcing or separating in acrimony after a year or two. Infatuation may be a first stage of falling in love, but it is never true love. It is full of self-seeking. And as soon as the infatuation disappears the relationship ends. The spousal language of the body, of making the sincere gift of self, was being misread all the time.

The non-verbal language of the body teaches us how to make that sincere gift of self, through which we discover our true selves and fulfil the meaning of our existence. That is a profound teaching. The notion that I can do what I like with my body is very alien to this view. If I want to live a fulfilled life I read the language of the body and live accordingly. I don't force the body to contradict its non-verbal communication. When

---

[26] *Theology of the Body*, 103:4.
[27] *Constitution on the Church in the Modern Word*, 22.

the body is speaking loudly about making the gift of self to the other, I should not be taking from the other. If I engage in self-seeking rather than self-giving I deny, in that very act, the fundamental meaning of the spousal capacity of the body. I no longer live in the truth of the body, but in a lie about the body – that the body is not made for self-giving, and not sacramental or pointing us to God. This distortion of the language of the body lies at the root of so much unhappiness. If my body is saying one thing and I am forcing it to do the opposite, the strain will tell. Happiness will elude me; fulfilment will escape me; peace will desert me. If I am not gratefully and peacefully living the meaning of my own body, nothing outside me will ever make me happy. And the meaning of my body is made very clear in John Paul's fundamental principle:

> The body, in fact, and only the body, is capable of making visible what is invisible: the spiritual and divine. It was created to transfer into the visible reality of the world, the mystery hidden from eternity in God, and thus to be a sign of it.[28]

The great gift that John Paul has given to the Church is to teach us how to see our bodies in a new light, in a sacramental light.

---

[28] *Theology of the Body*, 19:4.

Chapter Four
The heart as the battlefield for the goodness and holiness of the body

We have considered two fundamental categories that John Paul employed in developing his theology of the body. We have reflected on the body as the image of God and also as a sacrament. We have been developing the awareness that we don't just have a body – each of us can say, "I *am* my body." We identify ourselves through our bodies. As we do so we can hear more deeply the words of the Psalm, "You created my inmost self, knit me together in my mother's womb" (Psalm 139:13). When you were being formed in your mother's womb, God formed you as a body-person, an embodied spirit. What God created was very good and so you can say in your heart "my body is very good." And yet we are aware of a great struggle, an immense gap between head and heart, between the way we see ourselves in the light of God's word and the way we struggle to live up to our ideals. We desire to love and to be loved, to be fulfilled and live meaningfully and purposefully – to be happy. Deep down in our hearts we yearn for the holy, for wholeness and goodness, yet other desires rise up and seek to dominate our lives – the desire for power or indulgence in pleasure, or making ourselves the centre of the universe. St Paul was very aware of this inner conflict and he gave us his classic analysis:

> In my inmost self I dearly love God's law, but I see that acting on my body there is a different law which battles against the law in my mind. So I am brought to be a prisoner of that law of sin which lives inside my body. What a wretched man I am! Who will rescue me from this body doomed to death? God – thanks be to him – through Jesus Christ our Lord. So it is that I myself with my mind obey the law of God, but in my disordered nature I obey the law of sin. (Romans 7:22-25)

St Paul recognised that the struggle going on in his heart could not be won by his own powers. But where does this struggle originate? What explains the conflict we experience between the desire for the good and holy, and the failure to achieve our desire? We could ask, who or what put these noble desires for the good and holy in our hearts, and who or what put those contrary desires in our hearts? People who don't ask this question and yet seek an answer, often end defining themselves by their worst desires. They shrug their shoulders and say "I'm only human," as if that were a sufficient explanation for wrongdoing. But we would not define what it means to be human by reference to some disease, or the absence of health. If I have cancer I don't conclude "I'm only human." I know instinctively that I contracted the cancer in some way. Likewise, I should know that, in some way, I contacted desires or yearnings which are contrary to what is good and holy. The longing for what is good and holy and the yearning for the selfish and the self-centred are not equivalent, just as health is not the equivalent of disease. Yet both are found in the human heart.

Blaming the body

Far too often the body itself is blamed for conflict. Often good people complain about their sinful bodies, attributing their sinfulness to the fact that they are dragged down from the spiritual heights by their bodies. Nothing could be further from the truth of the Gospel. God became a human being, took on a human body, like ours in all things except sin, and rejoiced to live a human life. Jesus' human body wasn't an obstacle in doing the Father's will; it was the very means through which he fulfilled the Father's will. In fact, as we are told, Jesus said in coming into the world:

> You wanted no sacrifice or cereal offering, but you gave me a body. You took no pleasure in burnt offering or sacrifice for sin; then I said, "Here I am, I am coming," in the scroll of the book it is written of me, to do your will, God. (Hebrews 10:5-6)

It was through his human body that Jesus came to do the Father's will. We cannot attribute the origin of the conflict we experience in doing God's will to our bodies. We have to seek the explanation elsewhere.

The original sin

Deep down we want to do good and yet so often we do the exact opposite. As a result our hearts are troubled and confused. Jesus spoke directly to this confusion in the heart when he said, "Blessed are the pure in heart; they shall see God" (Matthew 5:8). Jesus holds out the promise of eternal bliss to the pure heart. Every heart, pure or impure, yearns for that bliss. The men and women whom Jesus is addressing in the Sermon on the Mount are those who live in the world that St John describes this way:

Everything that is in the world – disordered bodily desires, disordered desires of the eyes, pride in possession – is not from the Father but is from the world. And the world, with all its disordered desires, is passing away. But whoever does the will of God remains for ever. (1 John 2:16-17)

These disordered desires are more frequently called concupiscence or lust. That is how I will refer to them in this chapter. Concupiscence itself is not a sin. Rather, it is a strong inclination to seek sinful answers and quick solutions to life's challenges. This is the consequence of the original sin, the fall of our first parents, Adam and Eve. The Catechism explains it this way:

Man, tempted by the devil, let his trust in his Creator die in his heart and, abusing his freedom, disobeyed God's command. This is what man's first sin consisted of. All subsequent sin would be disobedience toward God and lack of trust in his goodness.[1]

That original sin robbed our first parents of grace and close friendship with God, but it did not totally corrupt human nature. The first Protestant reformers in the sixteenth century, as the Catechism points out, "taught that original sin has radically perverted man and destroyed his freedom." The Catholic Church always resisted the view that human nature had been completely corrupted by the sin of our first parents. But as a result of that sin all the descendents of Adam and Eve have been deprived of grace. The Catechism succinctly states the effects of that sin:

Adam and Eve transmitted to their descendants human nature wounded by their own first sin and hence deprived of original holiness and justice. As a result of original sin, human nature is weakened in its powers, subject to ignorance, suffering and the domination of death, and inclined to sin (this inclination is called concupiscence).[2]

The world that God created was "very good". By contrast, the world created as a result of original sin, was not. St John points out that lust does not only concern sexual pleasure, but also power and possessions: "Disordered bodily desires, disordered desires of the eyes, pride in possession – is not from the Father but is from the world" (1 John 2:16). It is the world in which each of us struggles because we have within us, as

[1] *Catechism of the Catholic Church*, 397.
[2] *Catechism of the Catholic Church*, 417-418.

a result of original sin, that threefold concupiscence. Blessed John Paul wrote:

> In fact, it is only *as a consequence of sin, as a fruit of the breaking of the covenant with God in the human heart* – in man's innermost (being) – that the "world" of Genesis *became* the "world" of the Johannine words (1 John 2:15-16), *the place and source of concupiscence.*[3]

Yet, it is the human heart, struggling in this world of concupiscence, to which Jesus appeals when he says, "blessed are the pure in heart; they shall see God" (Matthew 5:8). He calls us to that purity.

We know that there is a great gulf between the world of original innocence, into which Adam and Eve were created, and the world of threefold concupiscence in which their descendents now live. But Jesus has come as Redeemer and Saviour, the one who will bring new life and hope and power to the human heart and, consequently, he now both challenges and appeals to the heart to reclaim its original dignity and its original inheritance of innocence and holiness. Christ comes to restore our dignity.

A battlefield between love and lust

Men and women, despite the fall from grace, despite all our sinfulness, are still called to a life of communion with God and one another. The spousal meaning of the body remains intact, despite the sin. That spousal meaning can only be fulfilled in the communion of persons. It is precisely this dimension of communion that is distorted by sin. John Paul explains it this way: "Concupiscence as such is not able to promote union as a communion of persons. By itself, it does not unite, but appropriates to itself. *The relationship of the gift changes into a relationship of appropriation."*[4]

The inner nature of sin is always found in appropriating the other person for one's own use or advantage. Sin inflicts a deep wound, a painful alienation that seeks to paralyse the spousal capacity of the body which, as we have seen, is defined by John Paul as the human power to express love and become a gift, thereby fulfilling the meaning of human existence.[5]

---

[3] *Theology of the Body*, 26:2.
[4] *Theology of the Body*, 32:6.
[5] *Theology of the Body*, 15:1.

Our very power to love by making the sincere gift of self has been undermined and weakened by original sin. There is a struggle between self-giving and self-seeking in our hearts. Indeed John Paul refers to the heart as the battlefield: "The human body in its masculinity and femininity has almost lost the power of expressing this love in which the human person becomes a gift."[6]

He points out that he uses the word "almost" because: "… the dimension of the gift, the capacity of making the sincere gift of self, *has not been totally suffocated in it by concupiscence, but only habitually threatened.* The heart has become a battlefield between love and lust."[7]

Men and women want to love with a sincere self-giving love but now they experience something else going on in the heart, namely an urge to take rather than give, a yearning to possess rather than reverence, a desire to dominate rather than serve. The battle is underway. The moral life has become a struggle. The desire to be good remains, but the urge to act in a purely selfish way is very strong. That urge has taken up residence in our hearts, in the innermost core of our being, where we have the power to love, the will to seek the good, and the ability to know the difference between good and evil. But that lust does not destroy the image of God in us. No matter how often people fail and sin, as Pope Benedict says, "There remains in the depths of their being an ultimate interior openness to truth, to love, to God."[8] As we seek to enter into this openness within our hearts, we begin to experience new life. There is something much deeper in our hearts than sinful desire.

What has happened in the human heart is a tragedy because now human beings, with their strong desires for love and happiness, truth and generosity, have to struggle with urges contrary to their best ideals. Selfishness, self-centredness, using others for one's own advantage, abusing power over others – all these urges have somehow found a place in the heart. These urges or lusts "do not come from the Father." These concupiscent urges reduce the other to the status of an object – the very opposite of seeing the other as one to whom one makes the sincere gift of self. The heart has become confused. While it still yearns deeply for love and communion it often seeks the path of self-seeking

---

[6] *Theology of the Body*, 32:3.
[7] *Theology of the Body*, 32:3.
[8] *Spe Salvi*, 46.

rather than self-giving. That path leads to unhappiness, alienation and often despair. It leads to sin.

The illusion of happiness

It is the heart and not the body that has become sinful. Every sinful desire in the heart is not directly, as it were, a desire for something evil, but a desire for the appearance of what is good and promises to make us happy. Eve saw "that the tree was good to eat and pleasing to the eye, and that it was enticing for the wisdom that it could give" (Genesis 3:6). Concupiscence presents an illusionary good to the imagination, a distorted version of the good. Concupiscence is saying: *I want to be happy and if I do that, or get that, I will be happy.* The true self is saying, *I want to be happy and if I can make a sincere gift of myself to the other I will be happy.*

The concupiscent heart thinks that happiness is found in taking; the true, loving self knows that happiness can only be found in self-giving. The concupiscent heart, in its desire for happiness, may be saying, *If I swindle this person I will have the money that will make me happy.* Or, a man may be saying, *I no longer find fulfilment with my wife, but if I could have an affair with that beautiful woman I would be happy.* Instead of yielding happiness these actions instil remorse and inner pain: self-loathing rather than self-esteem. The amazing thing about human beings is that, no matter how often they discover that doing the wrong thing doesn't make them happy, they continue to trust their lusts. If you discover that somebody you're trying to do business with is a cheat or a liar, you will no longer trust them. Yet in personal matters, no matter how often the concupiscent heart fails to deliver its promises, we still trust the desires it puts before us.

Sin is really an illusion. It seems good, just as Eve saw that the tree was good, but the moment it enters the heart, the illusory good vanishes, our eyes are opened and we feel pain and remorse. What can we do then? Sadly many people give up hope of ever being able to love sincerely, or live truthfully, or act justly and honestly. They feel dominated by those selfish and disordered urges that we call concupiscence or lust. They surrender their very dignity to them and even identify them as signs of being human. Why would we identify our noble human nature with the ignoble disordered emotions that are within us as a result of sin?

The redemption of the body

Even Christians sometimes think Christ himself is powerless in the face of sinful human weakness. This is due, in large measure, to the neglect of a very basic dimension of the Gospel of Christ, namely the "redemption of the body" that St Paul speaks of. Blessed John Paul said:

> Redemption is a truth, a reality, in the name of which men and women must feel themselves called, and called with effectiveness… They *must feel themselves called to rediscover,* or even better, to realise, the spousal meaning of the body and to express in this way the interior freedom of the gift, that is the freedom of that spiritual state and power that derive from mastery over the concupiscence of the flesh.[9]

Sin is the failure to live the spousal meaning of the body, or to love by making the sincere gift of self. Notice the impoverishing consequences. Sin robs us of the opportunity to discover our true selves which, as the Second Vatican Council said, can only be discovered "in sincere self-giving."[10] Sin says, *take for yourself and be happy;* love says, *make the gift of self and you will discover your true self and be happy.* The true self is always happy and at peace no matter what is going on.

The heart, as John Paul said, has now become a battlefield. We struggle between self-giving and self-seeking. It is failure to exercise self-mastery in the face of concupiscence that results in the loss of the sense of the spousal meaning of the body. The person motivated by lust or concupiscence has surrendered self-mastery and even self-possession. He or she has only one aim, namely to possess the object of their lust, thereby reducing another person to the status of an object. The spousal meaning of the body means that the other person should never be objectified in this way. But we are not left to our own devices in fighting this battle. Through the redemption of the body, the saving grace of Christ, we receive the gift of "the new heart" and are empowered to regain self-mastery and self-possession. We have power in the face of concupiscence. We can live the spousal meaning of the body in all our relationships. But we need the redemption of our bodies. That is why Christ came. He said, "if the Son sets you free, you will indeed be free" (John 8:36). It is in that freedom with which Christ sets us free that we

---

[9] *Theology of the Body,* 46:5.
[10] *Gaudium et Spes,* 24.

can overcome the threefold concupiscence that St John speaks about. The Catechism confidently reminds us that, "The Spirit of the Lord gives new form to our desires, those inner movements that animate our lives."[11]

Realising the *entire truth* of our being

We should never identify ourselves through our lustful desires, no matter how strong they may be. And, no matter how strong they may be, we have redemption from them. In his encyclical on Christian morality, John Paul gave us Christ's answers to our lustful hearts:

> What are the concrete possibilities of persons? And of which person are we speaking? Of the person *dominated* by lust or of the person *redeemed by Christ*? This is what is at stake: the reality of Christ's redemption. *Christ has redeemed us!* This means he has given us the possibility of realizing the *entire truth* of our being; he has set our freedom free from the *domination* of concupiscence. And if redeemed men and women still sin, this is not due to an imperfection of Christ's redemptive act, but of their will not to avail themselves of the grace which flows from that act. God's command is of course proportioned to human capabilities; but to the capabilities of men and women to whom the Holy Spirit has been given.[12]

Christ empowers us to recover our dignity, reclaim our true capacity for love, and refuse to identify ourselves any longer by concupiscence or sinfulness. Christ knows that we are capable of greater things and he has come to show us the way. And his way is that of redemption. As he says, "I have come so that they may have life and have it to the full" (John 10:10). Christ's vision for us is to see us living his abundant life of love, realising the *entire truth* of our being in communion with God and one another. John Paul speaks the word of encouragement into our struggling hearts: "The words of Christ testify that the *original power* (therefore also grace) *of the mystery of creation becomes* for each of them *the power* (therefore also the grace) *of the mystery of redemption*."[13]

Redemption doesn't restore us to the state of original innocence. But Christ's redemption gives us the new life of the Spirit; it makes us "a new

---

[11] *Catechism of the Catholic Church*, 2764.
[12] *Veritatis Splendor*, 103.
[13] *Theology of the Body*, 46:5.

creation" (2 Corinthians 5:17). It restores to us the full grace that is ours as children of the Father; it makes us brothers and sisters of Christ. And to us whom he has redeemed Jesus says, as he said to Paul, "My grace is enough for you: for power is at full stretch in weakness." This inspired Paul to cry out, "It is, then, about my weaknesses that I am happiest of all to boast, so that the power of Christ may rest upon me" (2 Corinthians 12:8-9). In the battlefield of our heart, the deep yearning to make the sincere gift of self to the other will prevail against the desire of concupiscence, because Christ fights the battle with us. If we stay close to Christ we will win that battle.

Notice that lust attaches itself to the yearning in the heart for something much greater than power, sexual pleasure, or wealth of any kind. The yearning is for love, communion, truth and beauty, ultimately for God. As St Augustine said: "You have made us for yourself, and our hearts find no peace until they rest in you."[14] Lust in any of its forms is incapable of giving rest to the heart. If lust could fulfil the heart, then those who constantly indulge their lusts would be the happiest people on earth. But we know that's not the case. The heart is made for love and only true love can satisfy the heart. God created sexual pleasure, and the Church has always opposed the heresies that condemned it. If, however, the sincere gift of self is not made, sexual union is not a manifestation of love but of lust. It is not giving but taking, and the union is loveless. And loveless sex, no matter how much pleasure may accompany it, can never fulfil the heart. The sexual union itself looks beyond that pleasurable, physical union to a life of communion in faithful love and truth with one's spouse. The deep yearning in the heart is for that union in holiness and truth. Joy is the fruit of that loving communion of persons.

The inheritance of the heart

Experience teaches that, no matter how often a person seeks to satisfy some lustful feeling, it can never be satisfied. It cannot be satisfied because it is a distortion of the good. Self-seeking is not the way to human happiness; self-seeking is the opposite of true love which always consists in making the sincere gift of self to the other. In making that gift one discovers one's true self and becomes empowered for even greater love. This is the way of the heart responding to the call of Christ in his redemptive love. John Paul expressed this so well when he wrote:

---

[14] *Confessions*, I:1.

It is important that precisely in his "heart" he does not feel himself irrevocably accused and given up to the concupiscence of the flesh, but that in the same heart he feels himself called with energy. Called precisely to this supreme value, which is love. Called as a person in the truth of his humanity, in the truth of his body. Called in that truth which has been his inheritance "of the beginning", the inheritance of his heart, which is deeper than the sinfulness inherited, deeper than the threefold concupiscence. Christ's words, set in the whole reality of creation and redemption, re-activate that deepest inheritance and give it real power in human life.[15]

The inheritance of our heart which we have received from God our Father remains within us, even when we fill our hearts with all kinds of sinful rubbish. We remain the image of God even when our behaviour may be very un-Godlike. And Christ never abandons us to our sins. Our sins not only wound our own hearts and undermine our dignity, but they also break Christ's heart who died to free us from our sins. There is nothing Christ wants more than for us to come to him and ask for his help, for the cleansing water of the Holy Spirit to wash us clean. He said there is "rejoicing in heaven" (Luke 15:7) at the moment we come to him for help. When we open our hearts to Christ in this way the whole inheritance of our heart is reactivated. Let us remind ourselves again of the true nature of that inheritance:

- We have been made in the image and likeness of God (Genesis 1).
- We have sinned but have been redeemed (Genesis 3; 2 Corinthians 5:17).
- We are a new creation (2 Corinthians 5:17).
- We are precious in God's sight (Isaiah 43:4).
- We have been made little less than gods and crowned with glory and beauty (Psalm 8:6).
- We are reborn of water and the Holy Spirit (John 3:6).
- Our bodies are the temple of the Holy Spirit (1 Corinthians 6:19).
- We are God's work of art (Ephesians 2:10).
- We are the body of Christ (1 Corinthians 12:27).

As the inheritance of our heart is reactivated we become aware of the healing and renewing presence of the Spirit in our hearts. We reclaim

---

[15] *Theology of the Body*, 46:6.

once again our true dignity as the sons and daughters of the heavenly Father; we discover once again the joy of fully living the spousal meaning of the body; of true love in making the sincere gift of self. We no longer identify ourselves through sinful urges but through the word of God that reveals to us that we are still in the image of God, still precious in God's sight, and that God wants to fill us afresh with the Holy Spirit and set us truly free. The grace of conversion is being offered. If we accept it we will discover the transforming power of Christ in our lives. We will discover that, as John Paul said, redemption is indeed a truth and a reality.[16]

Informative or performative

There is no sinful situation that Christ will not utterly transform with his Holy Spirit when we open our hearts to his love. That was the whole purpose of his coming on earth, his preaching and teaching and ultimately his passion and death. Christ came to save us from our sin. As Pope Benedict said:

> The Christian message is not only "informative" but also "performative". That means: the Gospel is not merely a communication of things that can be known – it is one that makes things happen and is life-changing.[17]

And he asks each of us this very pertinent question:

> Can our encounter with the God who in Christ has shown us his face and opened his heart be for us too not just "informative" but "performative" – that is to say, can it change our lives, so that we know we are redeemed through the hope that it expresses?[18]

Our answer has to be an unqualified *yes*. Christ can do it and, as we open our hearts to him, he will do it. He will set our hearts free from the domination of lust. And once people have responded to the invitation of Christ, and tasted the freedom that Christ offers, they can joyfully accept the exhortation of Pope St Leo the Great, who said:

> Christian, recognize your dignity and, now that you share in God's own nature, do not return to your former base condition of sinning. Remember who is your head and of whose body you are a

---

[16] *Theology of the Body*, 46:4.
[17] *Spe Salvi*, 2.
[18] *Spe Salvi*, 4.

member. Never forget that you have been rescued from the power of darkness and brought into the light of the Kingdom of God.[19]

The pure of heart

Christ invites and challenges us with the words, "Blessed are the pure in heart: they shall see God" (Matthew 5:8). It is with our heart, the innermost self, that we can see God at work in our world. Scripture says, "To those who are pure themselves, everything is pure" (Titus 1:15). The pure of heart sees differently. And God promises that pure heart to each of us:

> I shall pour clean water over you and you will be cleansed; I shall cleanse you of all your filth and of all your foul idols. I shall give you a new heart, and put a new spirit in you; I shall remove the heart of stone from your bodies and give you a heart of flesh instead. I shall put my spirit in you, and make you keep my laws, and respect and practise my judgements. You will live in the country which I gave your ancestors. You will be my people and I shall be your God. (Ezekiel 36:25-28)

The deepest desire in each person is for this "new heart", this new power to love faithfully and freely, totally and fruitfully, throughout life. It is in our heart that we love by making that sincere gift of self. But it is also in our heart that we turn away from God and mortgage ourselves to sin. Jesus speaks of adultery in the heart. He said, "You have heard how it was said, *You shall not commit adultery.* But I say this to you, if a man looks at a woman lustfully, he has already committed adultery with her in his heart" (Matthew 5:27-28). Adultery is committed in the heart before it is ever expressed through the body. Here we have the new ethos of the Gospel. It is from the heart that both good and evil proceeds. It is the heart that needs redemption. So often the sinful desires of the heart are blamed on the body. That is why, in our Christian tradition, as Pope Benedict said, there has often been negativity towards the body.[20] The body is blamed for the sins in the heart, in the innermost will of the person. That is why Jesus challenges the heart. Christ knew the human heart, "could tell what someone had within" (John 2:25) and therefore knew that without salvation the heart was dominated by concupiscence.

---

[19] *Catechism of Catholic Church*, 1691.
[20] *Deus Caritas Est*, 8.

When Christ calls us to purity of heart he does so within his vision of redemption. As Blessed John Paul said:

> Such an appeal can be justified only by the reality of the redemption: outside of it there would, in fact, remain only the threefold concupiscence or that "slavery to corruption" about which the Apostle Paul writes (Romans 8:21). Only the perspective of the redemption justifies the appeal to the "beginning" or the perspective of the mystery of creation in the whole of Christ's teaching about the problems of marriage, of man and woman, and their reciprocal relation.[21]

Jesus is saying that we can live, in the power of his redemption, free from the domination of concupiscence. He is saying that he didn't come to help us cope better with the power of lust, but that he came to set us free from this domination. If we want to love truthfully and faithfully we have the power of Christ within our hearts to do so. But we have to make the profound decision to put true love, the sincere gift of self, before false love, seeking satisfaction or gratification for self. As Blessed John Paul says:

> In mature purity, man enjoys the fruits of victory over concupiscence, a victory of which St Paul writes, exhorting man to "control his own body in holiness and honour" (1 Thessalonians 4:4). He enjoys the "efficaciousness of the gift of the Holy Spirit" who restores to his experience of the body all its simplicity, its lucid clarity, and its interior joy.[22]

For this openness to the Holy Spirit we need to have our daily conversion. We have choices. We can seek what is true or what is false; we can put our own satisfaction before the good of others; we can treat others with respect and reverence, or we can use them as objects for our own advantage. In the heat of passion, that conversion will be put to the test. But Christian experience throughout the centuries enables us to say that those who consciously will to live free from the domination of lust, can do so with God's grace. John Paul preached this gospel with utter conviction, especially to the millions of young people who flocked to hear him: "*Christ has redeemed us!* This means he has given us the possibility of realizing the *entire truth* of our being; he has set our freedom free from the *domination* of concupiscence."[23]

---

[21] *Theology of the Body*, 49:3.

[22] *Theology of the Body*, 58:7.

[23] *Veritatis Splendor*, 103.

Through the redemption of Christ we become capable of living in the truth of our bodies: making the sincere gift of self with true and faithful love; never using or abusing another person for our own advantage or gratification. That is how we realise "the entire truth of our being".

The work of the Spirit

The Catechism says, "the Spirit of the Lord gives a new form to our desires, those inner movements that animate our lives."[24] The Christian way is not one of repression or denial, but of transformation. The urges that are contrary to true love, are renewed and transformed once they are surrendered to Christ and taken up in the Spirit. As the Catechism says, "Jesus came to restore creation to the purity of its origins."[25] This is our sure hope. And the grounds of our hope for restoration are given to us by St Paul who says, "For anyone who is in Christ there is a new creation" (2 Corinthians 5:17). Each day we start afresh. The motto of my Redemptorist Congregation is *Copiosa Apud Eum Redemptio* which means "With him there is plentiful redemption": more than enough for us all. And his gift of redemption comes to us in the gift of the Spirit who heals our minds and hearts. In the words of the Catechism: "Healing the wounds of sin, the Holy Spirit renews us interiorly through a spiritual transformation. He enlightens and strengthens us to live as 'children of the light' through all that is good and right and true."[26]

In that battlefield of the heart we are never alone. We can, therefore, live the spousal meaning of our bodies in joyful hope, knowing that Christ is with us to restore us and renew us in the Holy Spirit.

---

[24] *Catechism of the Catholic Church*, 2764.
[25] *Catechism of the Catholic Church*, 2336.
[26] *Catechism of the Catholic Church*, 1695.

Chapter Five
The spousal meaning of the body in the resurrection

Nowhere are we more in need of revelation than in the face of death, of physical disintegration. The Second Vatican Council said:

> It is when faced with death that the enigma of the human condition is most evident. People are tormented not only by pain and by the gradual diminution of their bodily powers but also, and even more, by the dread of forever ceasing to be. But a deep instinct leads them rightly to shrink from and to reject the utter ruin and total loss of their personality. Because they bear in themselves the seed of eternity, which cannot be reduced to mere matter, they rebel against death.[1]

Since God is eternal, and since we are made in God's image, we too must be, in some way, eternal. That is to have "the seed of eternity" within us. But we need the light of God's revelation to contemplate this mystery of our being. As St Peter said, the prophetic word is like "a lamp for lighting a way through the dark, until the dawn comes and the morning star rises in your minds" (2 Peter 1:19). Without the light of faith death is shrouded in total darkness and silence. It is the spectre at every feast. All the joy of living can be tainted or even destroyed by the thought of our own death, or the experience of the death of a loved one. Without faith we cannot stare into the face of death and see the new life of the resurrection. But with our faith in God's word we accept the truth that God abhors death. As the book of Wisdom says, "God did not make death, he takes no pleasure in destroying the living" (Wisdom 1:13). In his great encyclical, *The Gospel of Life,* Blessed John Paul said:

> The Gospel of life, proclaimed in the beginning when man was created in the image of God for a destiny of full and perfect life is contradicted by the painful experience of death which enters the world and casts its long shadow of meaninglessness over man's existence. Death came into the world as a result of the devil's envy and the sin of our first parents. And death entered it in a violent way, through the killing of Abel by his brother Cain.[2]

---

[1] *Constitution on the Church in the Modern World,* 18.
[2] *Evangelium Vitae,* 7.

But is death the end? That is the question that demands an answer in every new generation. It is a question that people of faith have answered in many ways throughout history. Jesus Christ gave the most definitive and indeed unexpected answer. He proclaimed the resurrection of the dead. And he offered his disciples the most compelling evidence for his teaching: he rose from the dead. The first proclamation of Christian faith was about the reality of the resurrection of Jesus from the dead. St Peter said on that first Pentecost morning:

> God raised this man Jesus to life, and of that we are all witnesses. Now raised to the heights by God's right hand, he has received from the Father the Holy Spirit, who was promised, and what you see and hear is the outpouring of that Spirit. (Acts 2:32-33)

In his opening lines of his letter to the Romans, St Paul said that the Gospel is about Jesus, "who, in terms of the spirit and of holiness, was designated Son of God in power by resurrection from the dead" (Romans 1:3-4). And he wrote to the Corinthians:

> If the dead are not raised, neither is Christ; and if Christ has not been raised, your faith is pointless and you have not, after all, been released from your sins. In addition, those who have fallen asleep in Christ are utterly lost. If our hope in Christ has been for this life only, we are of all people the most pitiable. (1 Corinthians 15:16-19)

The resurrection of Jesus from the dead is the core of our Christian faith. It has opened up a whole new dimension of human existence for us. It enables us to profess our faith in this way: "we believe in the resurrection of the body and the life of the world to come." In the light of our faith, the Church can pray in the Funeral Mass, "for your faithful people, Lord, life is changed, not ended."

The three phases in the revelation of the body

In his *Theology of the Body*, Blessed John Paul identified three phases in the revelation that Christ gives us about ourselves. We have the phase of "the beginning", of original innocence, when Adam and Eve, before their sin, lived in harmony and union with God. John Paul called this phase our *theological pre-history*.[3] We have no direct experience of what their life in the garden of Eden was like. We believe that our first parents lived a life of union and communion with God. That was God's gift to them.

---

[3] *Theology of the Body*, 4:2.

And God invited them to live this life for ever. But sin brought an end to this and, as God had warned them, death followed; "Of the tree of the knowledge of good and evil you are not to eat; for the day you eat of that, you are doomed to die" (Genesis 2:17). Ever since that original sin, human beings find themselves in the phase of "fallen humanity", experiencing our sinfulness, death and, most of all, the need for redemption from our sinful state. This is our *historical phase*.

Christ has redeemed us, has opened for us the gates of heaven. Now we can look with confidence to the final phase of human existence, to what is often called the *eschatological phase*, the phase beyond this life, in the life of the resurrection. If we limit our vision to the middle phase, the historical phase of fallen humanity, we will have only a partial view of what it means to be human. Without revelation that is precisely what we would have to do. We would be forced to conclude that the meaning of human existence begins with birth and ends with death. But, as the Church teaches, "Christ fully reveals humanity to itself and brings to light its very high calling."[4] Christ has revealed to us this other dimension of our human existence and so we can live in the joyful hope of eternal life and the resurrection of our bodies into a new existence in God.

The new dimension of the mystery of human beings

How can we talk about life after death? We know from our immediate experience of death that the body is placed in the grave or taken to the crematorium and that is the end of it. Or is it? Without the light of God's word we cannot face what is beyond the grave. But Jesus has spoken to us very clearly about eternal life, even about the resurrection of the body from death. John Paul says that, "Jesus has revealed a completely new dimension of the mystery of human beings."[5] Not everyone believed Jesus when he spoke about life after death or the resurrection of the dead. Among those who disbelieved in the resurrection of the body were the group known in the Gospels as the Sadducees, who were lawyers and experts in the law of Moses. They didn't believe in the resurrection of the body, nor in any afterlife or the spiritual world of angels. When they heard that Jesus was actually preaching the resurrection of the dead they engaged him in discussion. They produced a case aimed at showing the ridiculousness of any notion of a resurrection of the dead:

---

[4] *Constitution on the Church in the Modern World*, 22.
[5] *Theology of the Body*, 64:1.

Master, Moses said that if a man dies childless, his brother is to marry the widow, his sister-in-law, to raise children for his brother. Now we had a case involving seven brothers; the first married and then died without children, leaving his wife to his brother; the same thing happened with the second and third and so on to the seventh, and then last of all the woman herself died. Now at the resurrection, whose wife among the seven will she be, since she had been married to them all? (Matthew 22:24-28)

The Sadducees thought they had set a trap for Jesus. He would have to either disown Moses or change his own teaching. But Jesus' response showed them that they were trapped in ignorance of the scriptures:

You are wrong, because you understand neither the scriptures nor the power of God. For at the resurrection men and women do not marry; no, they are like the angels in heaven. And as for the resurrection of the dead, have you never read what God himself said to you: *I am the God of Abraham, the God of Isaac and the God of Jacob?* He is God, not of the dead, but of the living. (Matthew 22:29-32)

In telling the Sadducees that they didn't know the scriptures or the power of God, Jesus was making it clear that, as John Paul said:

Mere literal knowledge of the Scripture is not enough. Scripture is in fact and above all a means of knowing the power of the living God, who reveals himself in it, just as he revealed himself to Moses in the bush.[6]

The patriarchs were dead, in historical time, but in God's presence and eternal time, where there is neither past nor future, they are alive. While human beings, since the fall, are governed by the law of death, the creator is not constrained by this law. Those who are dead in historical time are living in God's eternal time. As Jesus said, "For to him everyone is alive" (Luke 20:38). That is the power of God that Jesus says the Sadducees do not know. Christ himself is God's final word on his power to give the life of the resurrection. Jesus said to Martha, "I am the resurrection. Anyone who believes in me, even though that person dies, will live, and whoever lives and believes in me will never die" (John 11:25-26). Jesus didn't introduce himself in that way to the Sadducees. They wouldn't have believed him. But Martha did. She replied, "Yes, Lord… I believe that you

---

[6] *Theology of the Body*, 65:3.

are the Christ, the Son of God, the one who was to come into this world" (verse 27).

The meaning of the body in the light of the resurrection

What does the doctrine of the resurrection teach us about the meaning of the body? Jesus says, "At the resurrection men and women do not marry; no, they are like angels in heaven" (Matthew 22:30). John Paul comments: "Christ speaks these words, *which have a key meaning for the theology of the body,* after having affirmed in the dialogue with the Sadducees that the resurrection conforms to the power of the living God."[7]

Christ makes it clear that marriage, the union that God willed in the beginning, belongs exclusively to this world, the historical world in which we now live, and not to the eschatological world into which we will be raised. In Luke's Gospel Jesus gives the reason why there will be no marrying in heaven:

> The children of this world take wives and husbands, but those who are judged worthy of a place in the other world and in the resurrection from the dead do not marry because they can no longer die, for they are the same as the angels, and being children of the resurrection they are children of God. (Luke 20:34-36)

John Paul comments:

> The words Christ spoke about the resurrection allow us to deduce that the dimension of masculinity and femininity – that is, being male and female in the body – will be newly constituted in the resurrection of the body in the "other world".[8]

In the life of the resurrection you will be yourself, the same person in eternity as you are now, but immortalised and divinised in your body. You will be able to say of your resurrected body, "I am my body", just as you are able to say today "I am my body." But we cannot say what kind of body we will be. We know from our faith that we will not be pure spirits, nor souls without bodies. We will be embodied spirits in the resurrection. St John says, "My dear friends, we are already God's children, but what we shall be in the future has not yet been revealed. We are well aware

---

[7] *Theology of the Body*, 61:1.
[8] *Theology of the Body*, 66:4.

that when he appears we shall be like him, because we shall see him as he really is" (1 John 3:2). We shall be like Christ in his risen and glorified humanity. That is our ultimate destiny, the reason why we are here. Our union with God will be eternally accomplished. This is truly the most amazing revelation of God, the greatest consolation of the light of faith, and it speaks directly to the deep yearning and desire in the human heart to be with our loved ones for ever.

Love doesn't die. Right now you still love your deceased loved ones, even though they may have died years ago. Your love holds them in your heart. God's love holds them in his heart too and God's love is creative and life-giving. In God's love everyone is alive and you too, after your death in this world, will be fully alive with God. That is the faith we profess every time we say "thy kingdom come" in the Lord's Prayer. Each time we say the Creed we proclaim, "We believe in the resurrection of the dead and the life of the world to come." And each time we celebrate the Holy Mass we act on the Lord's words, "Anyone who does eat my flesh and drink my blood has eternal life, and I shall raise that person up on the last day" (John 6:54). This gift of eternal life has already been given to us. In Christ, as St Paul said, "there is a new creation" (2 Corinthians 5:17). Commenting on the phrase "The Word became flesh" St Athanasius wrote in a letter:

> The human body has been greatly enhanced through fellowship and union of the Word with it. From being mortal, it has become immortal; though physical, it has become spiritual; though made of earth, it has passed through the gates of heaven.[9]

In Christ's resurrection our very humanity rose from the dead and is now "seated at the right hand of the Father."

Spiritualisation

In the resurrection we will be *like* angels, *not* angels. Our human nature will remain the same, but by becoming *like* angels a new spiritualisation will have occurred. Resurrection will mean the restoration of bodiliness, because the human person is an embodied being, not a pure spirit. We cannot speculate about what kind of a body the resurrected body will be, because God has not revealed this to us. But this doesn't mean that we should not contemplate this final reality of our existence, namely, our being raised to the new life of the resurrection in the glory of God.

---

[9] Office of Readings, 01 January.

That is our ultimate destiny. That is what deep down we yearn for. In every Mass we say that "we are waiting in joyful hope for the coming of our Saviour Jesus Christ." All the joys of this life are but a foretaste of the joy to come. God created us, not for eternal life in this world, but to be eternally with God in the world to come. To enter into this new and everlasting life we need the transformation and the spiritualisation of the resurrection (because of original sin we can now only come to this resurrection through dying in this world.) Blessed John Paul points out that this likeness to the angels will not be achieved:

> … through a disincarnation, but by another kind (one could also say, another degree) of spiritualization of his somatic nature, that is, by another "system of powers" within man. The resurrection signifies a new submission of the body to the spirit.[10]

We see this, of course, in Christ's own resurrected body. He was not limited by the limitations that our earthly bodies have. For instance, on that first Easter morning he appeared through closed doors. His resurrected body, which he invited the apostles to touch and feel, to assure them that he was not a ghost, had new capacities. Christ's body was fully permeated by the Spirit. New human energies and capacities became active in his resurrected body, which was fully spiritualised. But the spiritualised body remains totally corporeal. What we see in Christ's resurrected body is the human body, completely integrated into the new life of the resurrection. Indeed, Christ showed his disciples, as a sign that he had the same body, the wounds of his crucifixion. He said to his Apostle Thomas, "Put your finger here; look, here are my hands. Give me your hand; put it into my side." When Thomas professed his faith "My Lord and my God," Jesus responded, "You believe because you can see me. Blessed are those who have not seen and yet believe" (John 20:27-29).

Divinisation

In the resurrection, the human body will not simply be spiritualised, it will be fundamentally divinised. The children of the resurrection will be children of God, sharing fully in the divine nature. This is what we pray for in every Mass. As the priest adds water to the wine, during the Offertory, he says, "Through the mingling of this water and wine may we come to share in the divinity of Christ who humbled himself to share in our humanity." As John Paul says:

---

[10] *Theology of the Body*, 66:5.

Participation in the divine nature, participation in the inner life of God himself, penetration and permeation of what is essentially human by what is essentially divine, will then reach its peak, so that the life of the human spirit will reach a fullness that was absolutely inaccessible to it before. This new spiritualisation will be the *fruit of grace,* that is, *of God's self-communication in his very divinity,* not only to the soul, but *to the whole of man's psychosomatic subjectivity.*[11]

It will be our human body, made in the image of God, with its spousal capacity for mirroring the self-giving of God, that will be divinised.

In this divinised state, Jesus says, there will be no marrying or giving in marriage. Marriage belongs to our life on earth, to our historical existence, and not to the eternal life of the resurrection. Marriage is a sacrament, that is, a sign of divine reality. The union of man and woman in marriage is a sign of Christ's union with the Church and ultimately of the eternal union of Christ and all the redeemed in the kingdom of heaven. We will consider this in more detail in Chapter seven. In the next world there will be no marrying or giving in marriage. The human family will be complete. God's plan for the human race will be fulfilled. As the Catechism says:

For men and women, this consummation will be the final realization of the unity of the human race, which God willed from creation and of which the pilgrim Church has been "in the nature of sacrament." Those who are united with Christ will form the community of the redeemed, "the holy city" of God, "the Bride, the wife of the Lamb." She will not be wounded any longer by sin, stains, self-love, that destroy or wound the earthly community. The beatific vision, in which God opens himself in an inexhaustible way to the elect, will be the ever-flowing well-spring of happiness, peace, and mutual communion.[12]

The spousal capacity of the body is divinised in the beatific vision

In the beatific vision we will see God face to face. God, in that total mystery of being Father, Son and Holy Spirit, will communicate himself to each one of us, both individually and as a communion of saints. It will be that communication which will constitute the beatific state, the

---

[11] *Theology of the Body,* 67:3.
[12] *Catechism of the Catholic Church,* 1045.

state of complete human fulfilment. "It will be the definitive realization of God's plan to bring under a single head 'all things in [Christ], things in heaven and things on earth.' "[13] It is then that we will be truly and without fault in the image and likeness of God and, as the Psalm says, "crowned... with glory and beauty" (Psalm 8:5). On earth, historical men and women found this fulfilment symbolised in the sacrament of marriage, the symbol of the union of Christ and the Church. But in heaven there will be no sacraments and no need for symbols as we will see face to face. Our response in love to the God who gives himself so completely to us will be a completely beatifying response.

The spousal meaning of the body, as we have said, is the capacity to make the gift of self to the other and thus realise the meaning of one's existence. This means that, in the resurrection, totally spiritualised and divinised, we will have a new power to make that total gift of self to God. It will be on the basis of the spousal meaning of the body, in the life of the resurrection, that this beatifying gift of self to God will be made. In other words, the actualisation of the spousal meaning of the body, by the sincere gift of self to God in heaven, will be the expression of the definitive and total fulfilment of what it means to be a human person. We will be in the beatific vision of God. We are now at the heart of what John Paul calls "the revelation of the body". He says:

> This revelation penetrates in some way to the very heart of the reality we experience, and this reality is above all man, his body, the body of "historical" man. At the same time, this revelation allows us to pass beyond the sphere of this experience in two directions: before all else, in the direction of that "beginning" to which Christ appeals in his dialogue with the Pharisees about the indissolubility of marriage (Matthew 19:3-9); in the second place in the direction of the "other world" to which the Teacher calls the attention of his listeners in the presence of the Sadducees who say "there is no resurrection" (Matthew 22:23). These two "extensions of the sphere" of the experience of the body (if one may say so) are not completely beyond the reach of our (obviously theological) understanding of the body. *What the human body is in the realm of man's experience is not completely cut off from these two dimensions of his* existence revealed by Christ's words.[14]

---

[13] *Catechism of the Catholic Church*, 1043.

[14] *Theology of the Body*, 68:5.

Of course we need faith in God's revelation before we can enter into this kind of theological analysis. The originality and freshness of John Paul's theology consists precisely in the fact that he allowed his faith to go right into the depth of the revelation of the body given to us by Christ. His reflection began with going back to what God did in the beginning, in what he called our *theological pre-history*, and going forward to what God will do in the resurrection of the body, our *eschatological existence*. When we reflect on our human experience in our earthly condition, in the light of these two dimensions – the beginning and the end – we can, John Paul says, see, "*the coherence of the theological image of man in these three dimensions,* which come together in constituting the theology of the body."[15]

The theology of the body, therefore, cannot be formulated simply on the basis of our historical phase, our earthly experience cut off from the beginning and end. The analysis of the beginning is based on Christ's word, and the same applies to the eschatological end. Christ's word is addressed to us in our human, earthly situation. In our historical time we hear, as it were, what God did in his eternal time in the beginning, and what Christ will do at the end. Theology is always a reflection on the word of God as it is revealed to us. John Paul reflects in great depth on the word of God "in the beginning", in the creation of man and woman, on our "theological pre-history". He also reflects in depth on the redemptive word Christ speaks to the heart of the sinful men and women of history, on our "historical existence". Finally he reflects with great insight on Christ's word about the resurrection from the dead, on our eschatological existence. He writes: "Christ points out man's identity, although this identity *is realized in a different way in eschatological experience than* in the experience of the very 'beginning' and of all history."[16]

The spousal imagery of the Bible

The spousal meaning of the body will be fully divinised and realised in the resurrection. That power to make the gift of self totally to God will be permeated and imbued with the Holy Spirit. In heaven the spousal meaning of the body will enable us to enter into communion, not just with God, but with the whole of creation. We will be "the communion of saints". The spousal capacity of the resurrected and divinised body

---

[15] *Theology of the Body*, 68:6.
[16] *Theology of the Body*, 69:3.

will enable us to make the total gift of self to all. And God will "be all in all" (1 Corinthians 15:28). The spousal capacity of the glorified body will be totally fulfilled in our eschatological destiny. Scripture uses spousal language and images to convey the profound reality of life in the resurrection. There will be "the marriage of the Lamb" (Revelation 19:7): "One of the seven angels... came to speak to me, and said, 'Come here and I will show you the bride that the Lamb has married'" (21:9). The Church in glory, redeemed and sanctified by Christ, is the bride. The last chapter of the Bible closes with the prayer: "The Spirit and the Bride say, 'Come!'... Amen, come, Lord Jesus" (Revelation 22:17. 20). Of course this is an analogy. We speak about analogy when we use something very familiar to explain something unfamiliar. Jesus used his parables in this way. So, he would say, "the kingdom of heaven is like a mustard seed" (Matthew 13:31), or a net thrown into the sea (verse 47), or a sower going out to sow his seed (verse 3). The listeners understand what a seed or a net is, and from this understanding Christ invites them to visualise something of a totally different order. The image of marriage is also used in this way. In the Old Testament we are told that God will marry his people: "For your creator is your husband, Yahweh Sabaoth is his name, the Holy One of Israel is your redeemer" (Isaiah 54:5). John Paul points out that, "The analogy of spousal love and of marriage appears only when the 'Creator' and the 'Holy One of Israel' manifests himself as Redeemer."[17] In the Old Testament the love of the bridegroom for his bride is the image of God's love for his people. In the New Testament we are told that in the final fulfilment there will be the "marriage of the Lamb". Christ will be united with his bride, the Church, in an intimate union of love and friendship that in this world can only be compared to the love and union that unite husband and wife in holy marriage. In this sense we will all be the bride of Christ in heaven. Christ is the bridegroom and we are his bride. All our greatest mystics throughout Church history loved to contemplate this mystery of our union with Christ in this spousal imagery. But we have to keep reminding ourselves that this is analogous language. Just as the kingdom of heaven is like a mustard seed, so we can say our union with Christ in the resurrection will be like the union of bridegroom and bride.

Marriage on earth is a sacrament, a sign of the union of Christ and the Church. Even the happiest and most fulfilled marriage on earth, is not the final destiny of the happy couple. As Blessed John Paul says:

---

[17] *Theology of the Body*, 95:6.

Marriage and procreation do not definitively determine the original and fundamental meaning of being a body nor of being, as a body, male and female. Marriage and procreation only give concrete reality to that meaning in the dimension of history. The resurrection indicates the closure of the historical dimension. And so it is that the words "when they rise from the dead, they will take neither wife nor husband" (Mark 12:25) not only express clearly what meaning the human body will have in the "future world", but allow us also to deduce that the "spousal" meaning of the body in the resurrection to the future life will perfectly correspond both to the fact that man as male-female is a person, created in the "image and likeness of God", and to the fact that this image is realized in the communion of persons. The "spousal" meaning of being a body will, therefore, be realized as a *meaning that is perfectly personal and communitarian at the same time.*[18]

The resurrection opens up the new future to men and women, an eternal future, where God will be "all in all" and where the spousal meaning of the body will be utterly fulfilled through communion with God. The body, made in the image of God, has imprinted on it the creative and beatifying word, "self-donation". Living "self-donation" to the full, in our resurrected bodies in the next life, is the eternal destiny of each of us. The whole of creation is longing for this fulfilment. St Paul says:

> In my estimation, all that we suffer in the present time is nothing in comparison with the glory which is destined to be disclosed for us, for the whole creation is waiting with eagerness for the children of God to be revealed. (Romans 8:18-19)

As we come to the end of this chapter, we see the full meaning of the Church teaching, "Christ fully reveals humanity to itself and brings to light its very high calling."[19] Without this revelation we would never be able to look death in the face and look beyond the grave to our glorious resurrection.

---

[18] *Theology of the Body, 69:4.*
[19] *Constitution on the Church in the Modern World*, 22.

Chapter Six
Living the spousal meaning of the body in the celibate life

"Love is the fundamental and innate vocation of every human being."[1] With these words John Paul gives us a common lens through which we can look at our lives, irrespective of our various roles, positions, duties or talents. The Pope has a vocation to love; the milkman has a vocation to love; the Prime Minister has a vocation to love; the unemployed person has a vocation to love. It is love that gives meaning and purpose to life. We emphasised in the first chapter John Paul's view that life is senseless without love.[2] The way to a happy and fulfilled life is to love. As John Paul said, "happiness is being rooted in love."[3] The question that we now have to ask ourselves is: If love is the vocation of each individual what shape does it take in our lives? How do we embody a life of love? How do we live the life of love? Blessed John Paul writes:

> Christian revelation recognizes two specific ways of realising the vocation of the human person, in its entirety, to love: marriage and virginity or celibacy. Either one is, in its own proper form, an actuation of the most profound truth about men and women, of their being created in the image of God.[4]

In this chapter, following the order of John Paul's catechesis in *Theology of the Body*, we will consider the way of celibacy or continence for the kingdom of heaven, and in the next chapter we will reflect on marriage as the vocation to which the vast majority of God's people are called.

Nothing that Jesus said, in the hearing of his disciples, caused them greater concern than his teaching on the indissolubility of marriage. In his response to the Pharisees' question about the subject, Jesus pointed them to what God willed for man and woman in creation. In the context of that same discussion he proclaimed another vocation, that of continence. When the disciples heard his teaching on indissolubility they said, "If that is how things are between husband and wife, it is advisable

---

[1] Pope John Paul II, *Exhortation on the Christian Family in the Modern World* (1981), 11.
[2] *Redemptor Hominis*, 10.
[3] *Theology of the Body*, 16:2.
[4] *Exhortation on the Christian Family in the Modern World*, 11.

not to marry" (Matthew 19:10). In response Jesus spoke about a new vocation – new in the sense that there was no Old Testament tradition to fall back on. But he specifically made it clear that:

> It is not everyone who can accept what I have said, but only those to whom it is granted. There are eunuchs born so from their mother's womb, there are eunuchs made so by human agency and there are eunuchs who have made themselves so for the sake of the kingdom of heaven. Let anyone accept this who can. (Matthew 19:11-12)

The disciples would have known that Jesus had made himself a eunuch for the kingdom. And indeed, before his birth, his mother Mary had also chosen virginity for the sake of the kingdom (see Luke 1:35). This was a new departure within the history of the people of God, a new understanding of how to serve and love God with one's whole heart, and one's neighbour as oneself. In the tradition of Israel to be married and have children was the religiously privileged position, the only acceptable way of being a truly religious person.

A charism

Jesus was at pains to point out to the disciples that he was not imposing a new commandment on them. Rather, what he was saying would be accepted only by those to whom it had been given. And he concluded, "Let anyone accept this who can." He highlighted both the need for a personal call or grace, and for personal choice. Celibacy is a charism, a gift of the Holy Spirit, and to live a celibate life fully and joyfully means living a charismatic life, which finds fulfilment, not in marrying and bringing a family into the world, but in witnessing to the kingdom of heaven already present in the world. No one can live a life of celibacy for the kingdom of God without the grace of the vocation. Blessed John Paul comments:

> It is very significant that Christ does not directly link his words about continence for the kingdom of heaven with his announcement of the "other world" in which "they will take neither wife nor husband" (Mark 12:25). His words are found instead in the continuation of the dialogue with the Pharisees in which Jesus appealed "to the beginning", indicating the institution of marriage by the Creator and recalling its indissoluble character, which corresponds to the conjugal unity of husband and wife.[5]

---

[5] *Theology of the Body*, 73:5.

Christ links what he says about marriage with what he announces about another way of living life to the full, namely celibacy for the kingdom. He is speaking about a way of living in this world that will also fully fulfil the spousal meaning of the body and bring happiness. Blessed John Paul writes:

> *Continence* for the kingdom of heaven, *as the fruit of a charismatic choice,* is an exception with respect to the other state, that is, the state in which man came to share "from the beginning" and still does share during his whole earthly existence.[6]

Marriage is God's gift and way for the vast majority human beings. The charismatic choice of celibacy is, as John Paul says:

> *… a kind of exception to what is, by contrast, a general rule of this life…* It is not a question of continence *in* the kingdom of heaven, but continence *"for* the kingdom of heaven." The idea of virginity or celibacy as an eschatological anticipation and sign[7] derives from linking the words spoken here with the words Jesus was to speak in other circumstances, namely, in the dialogue with the Sadducees when he proclaims the future resurrection of the body.[8]

A new vocation

Jesus would have been very aware that the people he was addressing had no tradition within their own religious understanding to appreciate this new kind of vocation. That is why he begins by talking to them about eunuchs. They knew the reality of men who for reasons of physical defect could not marry. Leading on from their understanding of this, Jesus says there is a different kind of eunuch, one who voluntarily chooses not to marry for the sake of the kingdom of heaven. The motivation of the choice is central. Blessed John Paul makes this very clear:

> Even if it is consciously chosen and personally decided, continence without this finality does not enter into the content of Christ's statement… By speaking of those who have consciously chosen celibacy or virginity for the kingdom of heaven (that is, "made themselves eunuchs"), Christ emphasizes – at least indirectly –

---

[6] *Theology of the Body*, 73:4.
[7] See, for example, Second Vatican Council, *Lumen Gentium*, 44, and Pope Paul VI, *Perfectae Caritatis* (1965), 1.
[8] *Theology of the Body*, 73:5.

that, in earthly life, this choice is connected *with renunciation* and also with a determined *spiritual effort.*[9]

Motivation

The sole motivation for choosing celibacy has to be the kingdom of heaven. This can raise real questions about those who choose celibacy in order to be ordained. The choice must be directly related to the kingdom of God. The Church doesn't *impose* celibacy on priests. It will only ordain those who freely choose to remain celibate, for whom the choice is a joyful response to the charism of the Spirit, rather than simply meeting the canonical requirement for ordination.

While giving a diocesan retreat to priests on the theme Conscious Celibacy one priest said to me, "I never really chose celibacy for the kingdom. I chose it because I would not have been ordained if I hadn't. But today I am choosing celibacy for the kingdom of God." That priest joyfully welcomed the gift of celibacy.

The choice can only be made in response to the gift and call of the Spirit: "Let anyone accept this who can" (Matthew 19:12). In making this choice, the person opts for a new way of living that can only be sustained by the gift of God. Blessed John Paul says this option:

> … bears within itself above all the inner dynamism of the mystery of the redemption of the body (see Luke 20:35), and in this meaning it also possesses the characteristic of a particular likeness with Christ. The one who consciously chooses such continence chooses in some sense a particular *participation in the mystery of the redemption of the body;* he wishes to complete it in a particular way in his own flesh (see Colossians 1:24), finding thereby also the imprint of the likeness of Christ.[10]

Clearly the motivation of the option for celibacy has to be for the kingdom – that is, it has to be supernatural. It is not a pragmatic choice made in order to facilitate the freedom of movement for the sake of the ministry. Much less should it be for financial reasons – how could most parishes support a priest's wife and family? And it must be a choice informed by insight and understanding: "It is not everyone who can accept what I have said, but only those to whom it is granted" (Matthew 19:11).

---

[9] *Theology of the Body,* 74:5.
[10] *Theology of the Body,* 76:3.

The gift of self in celibacy

The spousal capacity of the body means that the person finds human fulfilment in making the gift of self and "discovers the true self".[11] Celibacy honours and facilitates this spousal capacity. The option for celibacy for the kingdom of God, while it excludes marriage and family, does not exclude the communion of persons which is established through making the sincere gift of self. The option of celibacy flows from the spousal meaning of the body, just as the option of marriage does. John Paul is at his best in showing the profound unity which exists between the two choices:

> On the basis of the same disposition of the personal subject, and on the basis of the same spousal meaning of being, as a body, male and female, there can be formed the love that commits men and women to marriage for the whole duration of their life (see Matthew 19:3-9), but there can be formed also the love that commits them for their whole life to continence "for the kingdom of heaven".[12]

The call to celibacy is a call to communion, but one that is not achieved as the communion of marriage is. It is, however, the same spousal capacity that makes both communions possible. Celibacy for the kingdom doesn't deny ones sexuality. It means that one's sexual being is fulfilled in a different way. Celibacy for the kingdom, or remaining single for Christ, is the way in which celibates choose to live out and integrate their sexuality in their human development and make a space where they can encounter God. Making the sincere gift of self, through which one fulfils the meaning of one's existence, doesn't require sexual union, but it does require true communion in love. Celibate love – unselfishly giving to the poor and needy, to outcasts and the sick, that celibates engage in – is a truly fulfilling way of life. Indeed, nobody is more fulfilled than the healthy celibate who is truly giving his or her whole self in the service of others. There is profound joy in this way of life. But the healthy celibate is realistic. He or she knows that the celibate life is impossible without the grace and strength of the Holy Spirit, just as it is impossible to faithfully live the full depth of marriage without it. We remain sinners in this life, even though we are redeemed sinners. The sexual abuse of young people by a small percentage of priests and religious, which has

---

[11] *Constitution on the Church in the Modern World*, 24.
[12] *Theology of the Body*, 80:6.

so shocked and shamed the Church, is a painful reminder that, without Christ's redeeming grace and strength, people cannot faithfully live their commitment. It is sinful human beings, not angels, who commit to celibacy for the kingdom. That is why Blessed John Paul says:

> It is precisely this person, in any case "historical" man, in whom there remains at one and the same time the heritage of the threefold concupiscence, the heritage of sin, as well as the heritage of redemption; it is this person who makes the decision by subordinating the sinfulness of his own humanity to the powers that flow from the mystery of redemption. He or she must do so just as every other person does who does not make a similar decision and whose way remains marriage. What is different is only the kind of responsibility for the chosen good, just as the kind of good chosen is different.[13]

Communion

The option for celibacy is not an option for loneliness or isolation. The person cannot flourish without being in communion. As John Paul says, "The dimension of the communion of existence is proper to the person."[14] Those who opt for celibacy for the kingdom, "have the awareness that in this way they can realise themselves 'differently' and in some sense 'more' than in marriage, by becoming 'a sincere gift for others.' "[15]

That gift of self for others which the celibate makes bears fruit in the kingdom of heaven. Indeed Blessed John Paul can say:

> … the spousal love that finds its expression in continence "for the kingdom of heaven" must lead in its normal development to "fatherhood" or "motherhood" in the spiritual sense (that is, precisely to that "fruitfulness of the Holy Spirit") in a way analogous to conjugal love, which *matures in physical fatherhood and motherhood* and is confirmed in them precisely as spousal love.[16]

True celibate love is always generative of new spiritual growth and life in those who are touched by it. In the sixth, seventh and eighth centuries the whole of Europe was evangelised by the Celtic monks who left

---

[13] *Theology of the Body*, 77:4.
[14] *Theology of the Body*, 77:4.
[15] *Theology of the Body*, 77:4.
[16] *Theology of the Body*, 78:5.

Ireland, in the freedom of their gift of celibacy, and brought the Gospel to many nations. In every English-speaking nation of the world in the nineteenth and twentieth centuries Catholic schools and hospitals, orphanages and nursing homes were established, staffed and run by religious congregations – celibate men and women who devoted their whole lives, out of love for Christ, to good works. They left their homes in Ireland and Britain, often at a young age, often never to return, and brought education and healthcare to millions. French, Dutch, Spanish, Portuguese and German religious were doing similar work in their own countries' overseas colonies. Their spiritual "paternity and maternity" cannot be counted. They built up the Church and brought immense benefits worldwide. The fruit of their celibacy for the kingdom of heaven is seen everywhere throughout the universal Church and the world. As Blessed John Paul said in his *Apostolic Exhortation on the Religious Life*:

> How can we not recall with gratitude to the Spirit *the many different forms of consecrated life* which he has raised up throughout history and which still exist in the Church today? They can be compared to a plant with many branches which sinks its roots into the Gospel and brings forth abundant fruit in every season of the Church's life. What an extraordinary richness! I myself, at the conclusion of the Synod, felt the need to stress this permanent element in the history of the Church: the host of founders and foundresses, of holy men and women who chose Christ by radically following the Gospel and by serving their brothers and sisters, especially the poor and the outcast. Such service is itself a sign of how the consecrated life manifests the *organic unity of the commandment of love,* in the inseparable link between love of God and love of neighbour.[17]

Bridegroom of the Church: bridegroom of souls

The person choosing celibacy for the kingdom of heaven should be motivated only by love: love for God and others, love in the service of Christ and the Church. This love is the heart's response to Christ's love for us. As Blessed John Paul says, following the great mystical tradition:

> *Christ himself is the Bridegroom of the Church, Bridegroom of souls, to whom he has given himself to the end (cf. John 13:1; 19:30) in the mystery of his Passover and in the Eucharist.* In this way, continence

---

[17] *Vita Consecrata* (1996), 5.

"for the kingdom of heaven", the choice of virginity or celibacy for one's whole life, has become in the experience of the disciples and followers of Christ an act of *particular response to the love* of the Divine Bridegroom, and therefore *acquired the meaning of an act of spousal love,* that is, of a spousal gift of self with the end of answering in a particular way the Redeemer's spousal love: a gift of self understood as a *renunciation,* but realized above all *out of love.*[18]

This spousal love for Christ is not consummated in a sexual way, as the spousal love of husband and wife is, but it achieves that communion of persons without which an individual remains lonely and isolated, and finds life meaningless. The spousal love of the celibate heart for Christ is blessed with that communion with Christ which is the gift of God. And in that communion the celibate heart is never lonely. If he finds himself on his own he knows this is a time of grace, a time for deeper union and communion with God. Jesus said, "Anyone who loves me will keep my word, and my Father will love him, and we shall come to him and make a home in him" (John 14:23). Intimate communion with the person of Jesus Christ, the bridegroom of the soul, is God's gift to those who choose and live celibacy for the kingdom of heaven. Pope Benedict develops this point:

> The fact that Christ himself, the eternal priest, lived his mission even to the sacrifice of the Cross in the state of virginity constitutes the sure point of reference for understanding the tradition of the Latin Church. It is not sufficient to understand priestly celibacy in purely functional terms. Celibacy is really a special way of conforming oneself to Christ's own way of life. This choice has first and foremost a nuptial meaning; it is a profound identification with the heart of Christ the Bridegroom who gives his life for his Bride.[19]

This insight – that choosing continence for the kingdom is an act of spousal love, an appropriate response to the spousal love of Christ for the soul – is solidly rooted in the Christian religious and mystical tradition. St Alphonsus de Liguori is a witness to this in his book on religious life, *The True Spouse of Jesus Christ*, published in 1760. Addressing consecrated religious, he says:

---

[18] *Theology of the Body*, 80:1.
[19] *Sacramentum Caritatis* (2007), 24.

> Cease, O spouse of Jesus Christ, to think of yourself or of the world; you belong no longer to yourself or the world, but to that God to whom you are consecrated... Your Redeemer and your Spouse has preferred you before all these; not because you are more worthy, but because he loved you more than them.[20]

St Alphonsus reminds his readers of what happens in religious consecration:

> A religious, on the day of her profession, is espoused to Jesus Christ; for in the ceremony of profession the bishop says to the novice about to be professed: *I espouse thee to Jesus Christ; may he preserve thee inviolate. Receive, then, as his spouse, this ring of faith, that, if thou serve him with fidelity, he may give thee an eternal crown.* Let us, then, ask the spouse of the Canticles who is this divine bridegroom. Tell me, O sacred spouse, what are the qualities of thy beloved, the only object of thy affection, who renders thee the happiest of women?[21]

Consecrated celibacy is a state of being in love with Christ the Bridegroom in a way analogous to the love a husband has for his wife. It involves the free and total gift of one's heart and soul, of one's whole being to Christ. If this gift is not being made in love, the celibate life loses its mystical and spiritual vitality. Without this gift, the celibate man would simply be a bachelor and his state of being unmarried would have no particular spiritual significance. Such a celibate life would remain unfulfilled because fulfilment can only be achieved through the gift of self, the activation of the spousal meaning of the body. As John Paul said, in the central thesis of his whole *Theology of the Body*, the spousal meaning of the body is, "*the power to express love: precisely that love in which the human person becomes a gift –* and through this gift – fulfils the very meaning of his or her being and existence."[22] The gift and charism of celibacy enables the person to fulfil the meaning of his or her existence in a new way.

Because the love that motivates the person to choose celibacy for the kingdom is a spousal love of Christ, John Paul can use his basic teaching on the spousal meaning of the body to analyse this religious commitment. Every decision the human being makes must conform

---

[20] *The True Spouse of Jesus Christ* (Brooklyn: Redemptorist Fathers, 1929), 36.

[21] *The True Spouse of Jesus Christ*, 19.

[22] *Theology of the Body*, 15:1.

to this spousal meaning of the body, because that is "the fundamental component of human existence in the world."[23] If we do not live in fidelity to the spousal meaning of the body we cannot be happy. It would be inconceivable that Christ would call anyone to a way of life that would necessitate the denial or repression of this. John Paul's theology unifies both the theology of consecrated celibacy and marriage. Both vocations are God-given ways for faithfully living out the spousal meaning of the body and thus living fruitful and fulfilled lives.

The spousal meaning of the body, revealed in Genesis, means humans, as male and female, exist *for* each other and are capable of becoming reciprocally a gift to each other. This *for each other* is at the basis of the communion that men and women are called to establish, especially in marriage. But Jesus shows us that this "for", which underpins marriage, can also be the basis of the choice of celibacy for the kingdom of heaven. Underlying both choices is the distinctive human reality of the spousal meaning of the body in its masculinity and femininity. A choice for celibacy cannot be made by ignoring or repressing this. The choice presumes a full consciousness of one's masculinity or femininity. As Blessed John Paul says, the choice, "is made *on the basis of the full consciousness* of the *spousal meaning,* which masculinity and femininity contain in themselves." And he adds a very challenging observation, "If this choice were made by artificially 'prescinding' from this real richness of every human subject, it would not correspond appropriately and adequately to the content of Christ's words in Matthew 19:11-12."[24]

The choice for celibacy requires a full awareness of the spousal meaning of the body, a mature recognition of the freedom of the gift, and the free decision to forego the good of marriage for the sake of the kingdom of heaven. There is no hint of the slightest negativity towards marriage in Jesus' words in Matthew 19:11-12, nor is there any basis for a doctrine of the superiority of celibacy. In one and the same breath, as it were, Jesus reaffirmed the dignity of marriage by appealing to the beginning, and proclaiming a vocation, given to some, to forego marriage for the sake of the kingdom of heaven.

These two ways of living the spousal meaning of the body, marriage and consecrated virginity, mutually enrich each other within the Church. The choice of celibacy contains in itself a reaffirmation of the dignity and the

---

[23] *Theology of the Body,* 15:5.
[24] *Theology of the Body,* 80:7.

beauty of marriage as a good that is given up for the sake of the kingdom of heaven. Marriage, with its biological paternity and maternity, reminds the celibate that he or she too must be fruitful in spiritual paternity or maternity. As John Paul emphasised:

> Marriage and virginity or celibacy are two ways of expressing and living the one mystery of the covenant of God with his people. When marriage is not esteemed neither can consecrated virginity or celibacy exist; when human sexuality is not regarded as a great value given by the Creator, the renunciation of it for the sake of the kingdom of heaven loses its meaning.[25]

Living the redemption of the body

Professing celibacy for the kingdom of heaven is a choice made not only in love, but also in the sure hope that what Christ invites us to do, he always enables us to fulfil. Christ's gift of redemption is not just redemption of the soul but also of the body. Consecrated celibacy witnesses to the redemption of the body in a unique way. John Paul warns against the "masters of suspicion"[26] who simply presume that the human being is incapable of living any of the Gospel values that the Church proclaims. They see the person only through the lens of lust, be it lust of the flesh, or for wealth or power. They don't acknowledge that the human being is capable of finding true self-fulfilment in sincere self-giving. In his great encyclical on Christian morality, John Paul says:

> Only in the mystery of Christ's Redemption do we discover the "concrete" possibilities of man... Christ has redeemed us! This means that he has given us the possibility of realizing the entire truth of our being; he has set our freedom free from the domination of concupiscence. And if redeemed man still sins, this is not due to any imperfection of Christ's redemptive act, but to man's will not to avail himself of the grace which flows from that act.[27]

A great scandal

A very great scandal in the Church today has been caused by some men and women, consecrated to God in celibacy, who have sexually abused minors. The horror of these crimes has caused immeasurable harm to

---

[25] *Exhortation on the Christian Family in the Modern World*, 16.
[26] *Theology of the Body*, 46:1.
[27] *Veritatis Splendor*, 103.

the victims and been a source of deep shame and agony to those who embrace celibacy for the kingdom of heaven. This terrible betrayal makes it clear that not everyone who feels called to celibacy is emotionally or spiritually capable of undertaking this way of life. In the formation process lasting many years, which priests and religious have to undergo, poor discernment of a candidate's suitability can take place. Great efforts are made to avoid this, but mistakes are made. This results in the ordination or profession of some men and women who are emotionally insecure and unfit, entering the Church's pastoral ministry, with tragic results. There is, of course, no excuse for sinning against innocent children. Paedophilia is an egregious crime, a deep sickness and a very serious sin. God alone can judge the sin; the state and Church have to deal with the crime and the sickness. Today the Church is galvanised as never before to deal with these crimes within its ranks. The abusing minority – and it is necessary to remind ourselves that this minority constitutes a very small percentage of celibate men and women in the Church – will never again be able to conceal their nefarious practices because of the new awareness and vigilance in the Church. Because paedophilia is a crime as well as a sin, bishops and religious superiors have a duty to refer all cases to the civil authorities.

In his letter to the Church in Ireland, following the awful disclosures in the Murphy Report, Pope Benedict addressed those who had been abused with these words:

> You have suffered grievously, and I am truly sorry. I know that nothing can undo the wrong you have endured. Your trust has been betrayed, and your dignity has been violated. Many of you found that when you were courageous enough to speak of what happened to you, no one listened. Those of you who were abused in residential institutions must have felt that there was no escape from your sufferings. It is understandable that you find it hard to forgive or be reconciled with the Church. In her name, I openly express the shame and remorse that we all feel.[28]

Every priest and religious knows the shame that Benedict felt. If a policeman or a doctor or teacher sexually abuses a minor in London, policemen or doctors or teachers in Glasgow don't necessarily feel shamed. But as members of the body of Christ, when a priest or a

---

[28] *The Light of the World* (London: Catholic Truth Society, 2010), 190.

religious sins against a young person in such an awful way, it inflicts a painful wound on the whole Church and every priest or religious feels shamed. We are brothers and sisters in Christ in the most profound sense. In the normal family, when one member commits a crime, all the family feels shame. It is the same in the family of the Church. At the same time it is important that we have a proper perspective on this appalling scandal.

Perspective

I have heard commentators, including priests, make the connection between celibacy and paedophilia. If that were the case how do we explain the worldwide plague of sexual crimes against children? In a World Health Organisation report[29] we have the shocking figures that in 2002 an estimated 150 million girls and 73 million boys worldwide were subjected to different forms of sexual abuse.[30] Will those who make a connection between celibacy and paedophilia make a similar connection between paedophilia and marriage? Paedophilia has nothing to do with being unfulfilled either in celibacy or marriage. It has all to do with human sinfulness and sometimes psychiatric disorders. As the John Jay Report on Sexual Abuse of Minors in the Church in the USA states:

> Mental health and treatment professionals have found that it is not uncommon for those who engage in child sexual abuse to demonstrate other behavioural and psychological problems as well. Studies on co-occurrence of sexual offending and other problems have consistently found high rates of personality dysfunction as well as major mental disorders such as anxiety or depression. Similarly, alcohol or substance abuse problems are frequently present among those who engage in child sexual abuse. Studies which have examined clergy who sexually abuse minors with co-occurring problems have found them to exhibit fewer psychological problems than other sex offenders. However, methodological limitations preclude firm conclusions about groups of clergy who offend.[31]

Priests and religious were so shocked and ashamed by the crimes of a small minority in the Church that they didn't try to get a perspective on what was happening. Anything we would say in defence of the celibate

[29] Geneva, 2006.
[30] www.zenit.org, accessed 23 May 2010. These figures are produced by Francesco Agnoli in his recently published book in Italian on the investigation of paedophilia in the Church.
[31] www.usccb.org/nrb/johnjaystudy, accessed 22 February 2011.

life would be construed in the media as a denial of the crimes. Any priest who wanted to link paedophilia with celibacy had instant access to both national and international media.

The John Jay College of Criminal Justice of the City University of New York was commissioned by the Bishops of the United States to conduct a study of all sexual allegations made against priests in the USA. From 1950 to 2002, 109,694 priests served the Church in America. In that period, 10,667 allegations were made against a total of 4,392 priests, or 4% of the total. The police were called regarding 1,021 priests, or 0.93% of the total; 384 were charged, resulting in 252 convictions, or 0.22% of the total; and a hundred priests, or 0.09% of the total number of American priests were jailed.[32]

John Jay gives us another perspective on these horrible crimes. Of the priests accused of sexual abuse, 59% were accused of a single allegation. 41% were subject of more than one allegation. Just under 3% were subject of ten or more allegations. The 149 priests who had more than ten allegations against them accounted for 2,960 allegations, or 27.7% of the total. This means that 0.13% of priests serving the Church in the USA over fifty years were responsible for 27% of abuse allegations against priests.

These statistics are of no comfort to those who have been abused. Many of them, as Pope Benedict sorrowfully acknowledged in his letter to the Catholics of Ireland, may still be locked in inner pain. But the Church in general, especially priests and religious who have felt the shame of what has been perpetrated by a minority, need to take heart and not be misled by attempts to blame these crimes on celibacy. The incidence of sexual abuse of minors by Catholic clergy or religious is no higher than that found among married clergy of the Protestant Churches, or other secular professional bodies – often it is much lower. Of course, not a single priest or religious should ever have sinned in this appalling way. And sometimes these crimes were totally mishandled by bishops and superiors. The Murphy Report on the abuse of minors in the Dublin Archdiocese, commissioned by the Irish Government and published in 2009, concluded that a "cover up" of clerical crimes had taken place.[33] This disclosure provoked great anger. The ordinary Catholic was shocked and

---

[32] www.usccb.org/nrb/johnjaystudy, accessed 22 February 2011.
[33] www.justice.ie/en/JELR/Pages/PB09000504, accessed 22 February 2011.

appalled. Some bishops had to resign. But as a result of these egregious crimes, and the public scrutiny of how the authorities dealt with them, no professional body today is more prepared to deal effectively with allegations against its members than the Catholic Church. They have learned from the serious mistakes of their predecessors. But the dark cloud of abuse has overshadowed the outstanding service that religious men and women have offered to the poor, especially in Ireland. Mark Anthony's words have a contemporary ring about them: "The evil that men do lives after them; the good is oft interred with their bones."[34] Justice for the tens of thousands of religious men and women, who gave of their lives in the service of their fellow citizens, demands that the evil done by the small minority doesn't have the last word.

The fact that I have to introduce this subject in this chapter on celibacy for the kingdom of heaven focuses my mind, once again, on St Paul's words: "We hold this treasure in pots of earthenware, so that the immensity of the power is God's and not our own" (2 Corinthians 4:7). We should never take God's grace for granted, nor presume to believe that we have in ourselves the strength to live the Christian life. As St Paul said, "It is all God's work" (2 Corinthians 5:18). The Catechism reminds us that, "Christ came to restore the original order of creation disturbed by sin."[35] And continues, "Jesus came to restore creation to the purity of its origins."[36] The man or woman seeking to live the celibate life for the kingdom of heaven has to remain close to Jesus Christ, otherwise he or she will be overwhelmed by the sinful weakness of fallen humanity. The threefold concupiscence remains in our sinful human nature. That is why Blessed John Paul says that the celibate:

> ... must *make this decision by subordinating the sinfulness of his own humanity to the powers that flow from the mystery of the redemption of the body.* He must do so just as every other person does who does not make a similar decision and whose way remains marriage.[37]

John Paul's *Theology of the Body* will provide for future generations an invaluable resource for the formation of those who are called to a life of celibacy for the kingdom of heaven.

---

[34] William Shakespeare, *Julius Caesar*, Act 3, Scene 2.
[35] *Catechism of the Catholic Church*, 1615.
[36] *Catechism of the Catholic Church*, 2336.
[37] *Theology of the Body*, 77:4.

Chapter Seven
Living the spousal meaning of the body in marriage

In the last chapter we reflected on the vocation to celibacy for the kingdom of heaven in the light of the *Theology of the Body*. In this chapter we will consider the vocation to marriage. Indeed, they have much in common. Blessed John Paul identified their shared source when he said:

> On the basis of the same disposition of the personal subject and on the basis of the same spousal meaning of being, as a body, male and female, there can be formed the love that commits man or woman to marriage for the whole duration of their lives, but there can be formed also the love that commits them for their whole life to continence for the sake of the kingdom of heaven. This is what Christ speaks about in his whole statement addressed to the Pharisees (Matthew 19:3-9) and then to the disciples (Matthew 19:11-12).[1]

In his consideration of marriage John Paul is simultaneously reflecting on the spousal meaning of the body, which finds fulfilment in making the sincere gift of self to the other, and also on the mystery of marriage as revealed to us by God. Marriage is the sign of Christ's union with the Church. John Paul loved to reflect on marriage as a sacrament of creation, what he called "the primordial sacrament", and as a sacrament of redemption instituted by Christ. But it is the same human reality. When the Pharisees asked Jesus, "Is it against the Law for a man to divorce his wife on any pretext whatever?" (Matthew 19:3) he asks them to consider that reality:

> Have you not read that the creator from the beginning, *made them male and female* and that he said: *This is why a man leaves his father and mother and becomes attached to his wife, and the two become one flesh?* They are no longer two, therefore, but one flesh. So then, what God has united, human beings must not divide. (Matthew 19:4-6)

Christ came, not to change what God did in the beginning, but to restore it. As the Catechism says, "Christ came to restore the original order of creation disturbed by sin."[2]

---

[1] *Theology of the Body*, 8:6.
[2] *Catechism of the Catholic Church*, 1615.

The sacrament of creation

We have been accustomed to using the word *sacrament* to identify the seven sacraments of the Church. But it has a broader meaning. A sacrament makes visible what is invisible. The grace and graciousness of God is invisible in itself but becomes manifest through signs. The first big and fundamental sign of God's grace and love was creation itself. God made the whole universe. As the Psalm says, "The heavens declare the glory of God" (Psalm 19:1). The term sacrament refers to how God reveals and communicates his grace to us. It is in this sense that John Paul speaks of "the sacrament of creation". Creation itself was the first revelation of God. God created the whole universe for us. "You have made him little less than a god... put all things under his feet" (Psalm 8:5-6). The grace of the sacrament of creation was lost through original sin. As a result, men and women have to struggle to make the sincere gift of self to one another. John Paul said: "The human body in its masculinity and femininity has almost lost the power of expressing this love in which the human person becomes a gift."[3]

Nevertheless, marriage remains at the very centre of salvation history. Paul's letter to the Ephesians calls marriage a great mystery (5:32). Even in our fallen state, it remains central to God's plan for our salvation. John Paul asks:

> Can we not deduce that marriage has remained the platform for the realization of God's eternal plans, according to which the sacrament of creation had come near to human beings and prepared them for the sacrament of redemption, introducing them into the dimension of the work of salvation?[4]

The union of man and woman in marriage is at the very centre, not just of the propagation of the human race, but also of the redemption of humankind. As John Paul says: "in the state of man's hereditary sinfulness, *marriage never ceases to be the figure of the sacrament, about which we read in Ephesians 5:22-23* and which the author of the same letter does not hesitate to call a 'great mystery'."[5] Whenever a couple truly commits to marriage, something holy is happening, something sacramental, even if they don't speak a religious language. Celebrating love is always

---

[3] *Theology of the Body*, 32:3.
[4] *Theology of the Body*, 97:1.
[5] *Theology of the Body*, 97:1.

sacramental because, as St John says, "Whoever remains in love remains in God and God in him" (1 John 4:16). That is why the celebration of a wedding is always the occasion for a feast. By God's design from the beginning, marriage is the "primordial" sacrament – the sacrament of creation. It is the union of man and woman, each made in the image of God, forming the communion of persons, which is the image of the divine communion of persons – the Holy Trinity. The bodily union of man and woman in marriage is capable of imaging the divine communion because, as Blessed John Paul said: "... only the body is capable of making visible what is invisible: the spiritual and the divine.[6]

Marriage, from the very beginning of creation, is God's design for his people. Indeed John Paul can say, "If we reflect deeply on this dimension, we have to conclude that all the sacraments of the New Covenant find their prototype in some way in marriage as the primordial sacrament."[7] For his magisterial exposition of the theology of marriage, John Paul reflects on the letter to the Ephesians (5:21-32). This magnificent word of revelation is the classic text for John Paul's profound reflection on the great mystery in all its dimensions. Sadly some people often know only one phrase from this passage, namely, "Wives should be subject to their husbands" (verse 22), and have never really looked at what St Paul is really saying. First of all, the scripture invites both husband and wife to be subject to one another "out of reverence for Christ" (verse 21). There is no prioritising the order of this – it is mutual and done out of reverence for Christ, who is at the heart of every marriage. Husbands are asked to love their wives as Christ loved the Church. How did Christ love the Church? He laid down his life for the Church. That is the model of a husband's love for his wife. The Christian husband says to himself "I will love my wife in the same way that Christ loves the Church." He is the first servant of his wife, just as Christ came to serve. For that reason scripture says Christian marriage reflects the love of Christ for the Church. But is this just too idealistic? It is if we don't accept the dignity of the human body, as the image, indeed as a sacrament of the presence of God. But, if we accept that our bodies have been made in the image of God, that we have the grace of redemption within us, we can begin to enter more deeply into this mystery of marriage.

---

[6] *Theology of the Body*, 19:4.
[7] *Theology of the Body*, 98:2.

Our eternal vocation

The letter to the Ephesians begins with the mystery of God's eternal choice of us: "Thus he chose us in Christ before the world was made to be holy and faultless before him in love, marking us out for himself beforehand, to be adopted sons, through Jesus Christ" (1:4-5). The letter reveals to us our very origins in the mystery of God. We are in the world of faith, personal faith, that light which enables us to say, "Yes, Lord, I believe." Without this faith much of what John Paul teaches on the holiness of marriage will be lost. He points out that the passage on marriage comes:

> … at the intersection of the *two main guiding lines* of the whole letter to the Ephesians: the first is the mystery of Christ which is realized in the Church as an expression of the divine plan for man's salvation; the second is the Christian vocation as the model of the baptized persons and particular communities, corresponding to the mystery of Christ or to the divine plan for the salvation of man.[8]

Being called to be holy and predestined to be children of God our lives have to reflect this extraordinary grace that is given to us. So the writer lists the duties that flow from being in Christ, and he concludes with the great encouragement to spiritual battle, Ephesians 6:10-20.

Speaking directly to husbands and wives, St Paul says, "Be subject to one another out of reverence for Christ" (Ephesians 5:21). It is their mutual relationship with Christ which determines their relationship with one another. As John Paul says, "Husband and wife, are, in fact 'subject to one another', mutually subordinated to one another. *The source* of this reciprocal submission lies in the Christian *pietas* and *its expression is love*."[9]

The great analogy

The model of the spouses' relationship is based on Christ's relationship with the Church. This is the great analogy. As Christ loves the Church, husbands should love their wives; as the Church is subject to Christ, so the wife should be subject to her husband, but understood in the light of being subject to one another. Blessed John Paul comments:

---

[8] *Theology of the Body*, 88:3.
[9] *Theology of the Body*, 89:3.

The whole text of Ephesians 5:21-23 is permeated by the same analogy: that is, the reciprocal relationship between the spouses, husband and wife, should be understood by Christians *according to the image of the relationship between Christ and the Church*.[10]

In Christian marriage the husband doesn't dominate his wife. Such domination is seen in Genesis as the direct result of original sin. The couple who are in Christ are new beings.

The great analogy in Ephesians, namely love of husband and wife mirroring the love of Christ for the Church and vice versa, throws light on both Christ's relationship with the Church and also on the nature of Christian marriage. It is, however, an *analogy*, not an exact replica. Marriage is like the union of Christ and the Church, but it is not the same kind of union. In analogies there are always greater dissimilarities than similarities. "Analogy" is defined in the *Oxford English Dictionary* as a "process of arguing from similarity in known respects to similarity in other respects." The great analogy in Ephesians is based on similarity, but we should remember that there is greater dissimilarity between the "one-flesh" union, that is the love between husband and wife, and the union between Christ and the Church.

The transforming grace of marriage

The great analogy is a fundamental revelation from God. As Blessed John Paul says:

> While the analogy used in Ephesians clarifies the mystery of the relationship between Christ and the Church, at the same time *it reveals the essential truth about marriage,* namely, that marriage corresponds to the vocation of Christians only when it mirrors the love that Christ, the Bridegroom, gives to the Church, his Bride, and which the Church (in likeness to the wife who is "subject", and thus completely given) seeks to give back to Christ in return. This is the redeeming, saving love, the love with which men and women have been loved by God from eternity in Christ.[11]

The mystery and dignity of marriage consists precisely in this – that the married couple have within them, through the sacrament of marriage,

---

[10] *Theology of the Body*, 89:3.
[11] *Theology of the Body*, 90:2.

the grace to image or mirror the love of Christ for the Church. That is the transforming grace of Christian marriage – the couple no longer have to depend simply on their own love, for they now have the very love of Christ at the heart of their love. And the love of Christ will never fail them. The great analogy, as Blessed John Paul says, "shows us in some sense the way in which this marriage, in its deepest essence, *emerges from the mystery* of God's eternal love for man and humanity: from the salvific mystery that Christ's spousal love fulfils in time for the Church."[12]

Christ loves the Church with such a total self-giving love that he laid down his life for her; this is the model of the husband's love for his wife when they live in reverence for Christ, and in reciprocal submission. Selfishness is the very opposite of this kind of love. A marriage built on self-giving love lasts, but a marriage built of selfishness will begin to crumble.

The redemption of the body

Christ speaks from the depths of the divine mystery of the redemption of the body which he accomplishes in and for us. His words are addressed, not just to us in our sinful weakness, but also to the "inheritance of the Father"[13] which is within us, in our hearts, even though it may be deeply buried by our sinfulness. For this reason we say Christ never asks the impossible of us. What may seem impossible from the perspective of sinfulness becomes possible within the perspective of the redemption of the body. As Blessed John Paul said:

> Redemption is a truth, a reality, in the name of which men and women must feel themselves called, and called with effectiveness... They *must feel themselves called to rediscover,* or even better, to realise, the spousal meaning of the body and to express in this way the interior freedom of the gift, that is the freedom of that spiritual state and power that derive from mastery over the concupiscence of the flesh.[14]

We are very aware that our sinfulness can be destructive of our relationships. We can suffer from jealousy and possessiveness, rancour and bitterness, selfish, lustful desires and blindness to our own faults. That is why so many marriages that began with celebration and joy end in tears and pain. But they don't have to. Christ has redeemed the most broken part of each of us. He wants to heal all our wounds.

---

[12] *Theology of the Body*, 4.
[13] See also Chapter 4, and *Theology of the Body*, 44:6.
[14] *Theology of the Body*, 46:5.

The heart of marriage

The heart of marriage as a human reality is the love of husband and wife. In their marriage the gift of self is made in such a profound way that that the two become one, one subject, a "we" instead of two "I"s. The gift of self, lived and expressed through the body, is total, truthful, faithful and fruitful. It is not made *through* the body, as if the physical being were simply a means for delivery, but not the self. As we have seen throughout this exploration of John Paul's theology, *the body is personal*. The self necessarily means the body and everything about it, because the self is a body-person, an "incarnated-person".[15] John Paul says:

> The body, which expresses femininity "for" masculinity and vice versa, manifests the reciprocity of the communion of persons. It expresses it through gift as the fundamental characteristic of existence. This is *the body: a witness* to creation as a fundamental gift, and therefore a witness *to Love as the source from which this same giving springs.* Masculinity-femininity – namely, sex – is the original sign of a creative donation and at the same time the sign of a gift that man, male-female, becomes aware of as a gift lived so to speak in an original way. This is the meaning with which sex enters into the theology of the body.[16]

Receiving the gift of self and the body in sexual intercourse, means that the two become one – and it has a meaning that is both unitive and procreative.

The language of the body

As a witness to love the body speaks its own language of love. The body speaks its own truth that the gift of self in sexual intercourse is total and faithful, fruitful and forever. Each time husband and wife become one they are ratifying their marriage vows. At the altar on their wedding day the priest asks the couple: "Do you take ___ as your lawful wife/husband, to have and to hold, from this day forward, for better or for worse, for richer or for poorer, in sickness and in health, to love and cherish until death do you part?" In every act of sexual intercourse the couple live out this promise of loving and cherishing each other. Blessed John Paul says:

---

[15] *Theology of the Body*, 69:8.
[16] *Theology of the Body*, 14:4.

As ministers of the sacrament that is constituted through consent and perfected by conjugal union, man and woman are called *to* express the mysterious *"language" of their bodies in all the truth that properly belongs to it.* Through gestures and reactions, through the whole reciprocally conditioned dynamism of tension and enjoyment – whose direct source is the body in its masculinity and femininity, the body in its action and interaction – through all this *man, the person,* speaks.[17]

The joy, the pleasure, the ecstasy which they experience in making love sanctifies them and gives glory to God. It is not only a time of sexual love, communion and fulfillment; it is a sacramental moment, a moment of grace in which their human love is filled with Christ's love. When husband and wife become one through their sexual union a sacramental reality is being celebrated. Their love for each other is an image of Christ's love for the Church. As St Paul said, it is a mystery that has great significance, that can be applied to the Church (Ephesians 5:31). This faith enhances the joy of their sexual union. They know that God is blessing them and the love, intimacy and delight they experience in one another is God's gift to them.

God created the joy of sexual union so that husband and wife can grow in love, sharing the pleasure that God has created for them. As a young priest and professor of ethics in Poland, thirty years before he became Pope, Karol Wojtyla had an amazing community of young men and women, all university students, who gathered to discuss theological and moral issues, to pray and celebrate the Mass, and to hike and ski and kayak. These students became his close friends and he became their confidant. The group was known by the Polish name, *Stodowisko.* One member recalled: "While he was among us, we felt that we could discuss any problem with him: we could talk about absolutely anything."[18] A topic that always came up and which they discussed in great depth was the nature of true love, especially of married love. His first major book, *Love and Responsibility*, published twenty years before he became Pope, emerged from this profound sharing with young married couples. No celibate theologian ever had such an education in the challenges and beauty of married life. I quote just one observation:

---

[17] *Theology of the Body*, 123:4.

[18] George Weigel, *The End and the Beginning Pope John Paul II – The Victory of Freedom, the Last Years, the Legacy* (New York: Doubleday, 2010), 41.

The man must take the difference between male and female reactions into account, not for hedonistic but for altruistic reasons. There exists a rhythm dictated by nature itself which both spouses must discover so that climax may be reached both by the man and by the woman, and as far as possible occur in both simultaneously. The subjective happiness which they then share has the clear characteristic of the enjoyment which we have called *frui* (Latin for "to enjoy"), of the joy which flows from harmony between one's own actions and the objective order of nature. Egoism on the other hand – is inseparable from the *uti* (Latin for "to use") in which one party seeks only his own pleasure at the expense of the other.[19]

The act of sexual intercourse in marriage is the holiest action husband and wife can perform. That gift of self remains even when the passion abates. But if it is not sincerely given, despite the sexual pleasure, there will be a sense of emptiness. The body knows the difference. As Blessed John Paul says:

This spiritual understanding is the fundamental fruit of the gift of the Spirit that impels the person to reverence for the work of God. It is from this understanding, and thus indirectly from this gift, that all the "affective manifestations" that form the fabric of the stability of conjugal union draw true spousal meaning. This union is expressed through the conjugal act only in some circumstances, but it can and should be manifested continually, every day, through the various "affective manifestations" that are shaped by the power of a "disinterested" emotion of the "I" in relation to femininity and reciprocally in relation to masculinity.[20]

By "'disinterested' emotion" John Paul means that the person is loving the other for his or her sake and not just for personal satisfaction.

The body speaks its own language. In the act of sexual intercourse the bodies of husband and wife are saying: We have become one flesh. There is no personal act of loving which is not at the same time both physical and spiritual. Pope Benedict expresses the Church's tradition clearly when he writes:

It is neither the spirit alone nor the body alone that loves; it is the person, a unified creature composed of body and soul, who loves.

---

[19] *Love and Responsibility*, 272.
[20] *Theology of the Body*, 132:4.

Only when both dimensions are truly united, does the person attain his or her full stature. Only thus is love – *eros* – able to mature and attain authentic grandeur.[21]

Up until the 1930s every Christian Church proclaimed the doctrine of the inviolable unity of the procreative and unitive dimension of sexual intercourse in marriage. Then, at the 1930 Lambeth Conference, the Anglican Church changed its teaching. It left the issue open to the consciences of couples. Other Protestant Churches quickly followed suit. The Catholic Church came under great pressure, especially with the introduction of the pill, to follow suit. But instead, Pope Paul VI restated the Church's traditional doctrine in 1968, and said that the procreative and unitive dimensions of the act of intercourse cannot morally be separated. He summed up the Catholic tradition:

> The Church teaches that each and every marriage act must remain through itself open to the transmission of life. That teaching... is founded upon the indissoluble connection, willed by God and unable to be broken by man on his own initiative, between the two meanings of the conjugal act: the unitive meaning and the procreative meaning. Indeed by its intimate structure, the conjugal act, while most closely uniting husband and wife, capacitates them for the generation of new lives, according to laws inscribed in the very being of man and woman. By safeguarding both these essential aspects, the unitive and procreative, the conjugal act preserves in its fullness the sense of true mutual love and its ordination towards man's most high calling to parenthood.[22]

The sexual "revolution" was in full swing in 1968, and Pope Paul's encyclical was met with fury and derision by many commentators, including some Catholics. For him, the Church's stance that sex outside marriage is wrong, would be untenable if the Catholic Church approved of contraceptive practices in marriage. Despite pressure from without and challenges from within, this still describes the magisterial position of the Catholic Church. As Pope Benedict has written: "If we separate sexuality and fecundity from each other in principle, which is what the use of the pill does, then sexuality becomes arbitrary. Logically, every form of sexuality is of equal value."[23]

---

[21] *Deus Caritas Est*, 5.

[22] Pope Paul VI, *Humanae Vitae* (1968), 12.

[23] *The Light of the World*, 146.

But this is not simply a view that has been imposed on Catholic people. It's striking how many Catholics (and, indeed, non-Catholics and non-religious people) share the Church's deep concerns about the division between the unitive and procreative aspects of the conjugal act. They suspect that this division has had widespread and disastrous consequences for many individuals and for society as a whole, and has been responsible for countless broken marriages and abortions, and an epidemic of sexually transmitted diseases.

Blessed John Paul in his encyclical *On the Family* writes:

> In the light of the experience of many couples and of the data provided by the different human sciences, theological reflection is able to perceive and is called to study further the difference, both anthropological and moral, between contraception and recourse to the rhythm of the cycle: it is a difference which is much wider and deeper than is usually thought, one which involves in the final analysis two irreconcilable concepts of the human person and of human sexuality.[24]

Many couples – both Christian and non-Christian – who have chosen to live their sexual lives in harmony with the natural rhythms of the body say they find it enriching, and experience deeper joy and intimacy. Great developments have taken place in the approach of natural family planning methods in the past fifty years, and many people find it makes all the difference between respecting the body's fertile rhythms, or suppressing or blocking fertility.

The *Theology of the Body*, with its clear focus on the spousal and sacramental meaning of the body, provides the explanation as to this enrichment of marriage and family life. As John Paul said, we are faced with "two irreconcilable concepts of the human person and of human sexuality."[25] There is the utilitarian view that sees the body as an object for pleasure. And there is the personalistic view that sees the body as the embodied spirit, full of the dignity of the human person. In the utilitarian view one can manipulate the body in any way one chooses to maximise pleasure. In the personalistic view one never treats the body as an object. Blessed John Paul was the great defender of human dignity in every area of life, but especially the dignity of the body and the reverence that

---

[24] *Familiaris Consortio*, 32.
[25] *Familiaris Consortio*, 32.

husband and wife have for each other. Married theologian Don Asci captures John Paul's teaching well when he writes:

> According to Catholic teaching, the conjugal act incorporates the language of the body and its spousal meaning, the potential for parenthood, and man's capacity for co-subjectivity and friendship… In its personal dimension, the conjugal act enables husband and wife to fulfil their fundamental vocation to form a loving personal communion in accord with their identity as the image and likeness of the Triune God. By viewing the conjugal act as a personal act, the Church promotes both the dignity of the act and the dignity of the person.[26]

St Paul gives us the vision for living in the truth of our bodies. He writes:

> God wills you all to be holy. He wants you to keep away from sexual immorality, and each of you to know how to control his body in a way that is holy and honourable, not giving way to selfish lust like *the nations who do not acknowledge God*. He wants nobody at all ever to sin by taking advantage of a brother or sister in these matters… God called us to be holy, not to be immoral. (1 Thessalonians 4:3-7)

Living in the truth of our bodies means living in reverence for our own body and relating to others with that same reverence. The whole vision of the *Theology of the Body* convinces us that reverence for the body is reverence for the person, and ultimately for God. Living in the truth of the body means living the life of love and never using another person for one's own advantage. Pope Benedict made this very clear when he said: "Human nature, in its most profound essence, consists in loving. In a word, only one task is entrusted to every human being: to learn to will the good, to love, sincerely, authentically, freely."[27]

Morality and the redemption of the body

We cannot truthfully proclaim Christian morality if we do not at the same time proclaim the liberating power of Christ, who is absent from no one. As the Vatican Council said, "By his incarnation the Son of God

---

[26] Donald P. Asci , *The Conjugal Act as a Personal Act: A Study of the Catholic Concept of the Conjugal Act in the Light of Christian Anthropology* (San Francisco: Ignatius Press, 2002), 331.

[27] www.zenit.org, accessed 02 December 2009.

has in a certain way united himself with each individual… we must hold that the Holy Spirit offers to all the possibility of being made partners, in a way known to God, in the paschal mystery."[28] People who have never experienced the redemption of the body, even though they may be nominally Christian, genuinely believe that Christian morality is impossible to live. I have often heard people say, sadly even priests: You can't expect the ordinary person to live according to the Church's teaching on contraception or sex outside marriage. John Paul was aware that without Christ we cannot live Christian morality. He wrote:

> Through redemption, every human being has received himself and his own body anew, as it were, from God… *The redemption of the body* brings with it the establishment in Christ and for Christ of a new *measure of holiness of the body*. Paul appeals to this holiness when he writes in 1 Thessalonians that one should "keep one's own body with holiness and reverence."[29]

Without redemption, without the presence of Christ's grace or the power of the Holy Spirit, it is impossible to live in the truth of our bodies, in the Spirit. But in the power of the Holy Spirit, through the grace of Christ, Christian morality is the way of human dignity and leads to a rich and joyful fulfilment of human life. In his great encyclical on Christian morality, John Paul said:

> Love and life according to the Gospel cannot be thought of first and foremost as a kind of precept, because what they demand is beyond man's abilities. They are possible only as a result of a gift of God who heals, restores, and transforms the human heart by his grace… We are speaking of *a possibility opened to men and women exclusively by grace,* by the gift of God, by his love.[30]

Pope Benedict reaffirmed this truth in his first encyclical when he wrote: "Being Christian is not the result of an ethical choice or a lofty idea, but the encounter with a person, which gives life a new horizon and a decisive direction."[31]

When we speak about living in the truth of our bodies, living Christian morality, especially in intimate relationships, it's important to keep in

---

[28] *Gaudium et Spes*, 22.
[29] *Theology of the Body*, 56:5
[30] *Veritatis Splendor*, 23, 24.
[31] *Deus Caritas Est*, 1.

mind the fact that only the encounter with Christ can make Christian morality liveable because Christ alone "can fully reveal humanity to itself and bring to light its very high calling."[32] Our starting point in understanding ourselves is the revelation that, although we have been made in the image and likeness of God, we lost God's grace through the original sin of our first parents and our own sins, and now each one of us is in need of salvation. As Blessed John Paul said:

> *Christ has redeemed us!* This means that he has given us the possibility of realising *the entire* truth of our being; he has set our freedom free from the *domination* of concupiscence. And if the redeemed person still sins, this is not due to an imperfection of Christ's redemptive act, but to the person's will not to avail of the grace which flows from that act.[33]

Living in the truth of the body is only possible when we live life in Christ in the power of the Holy Spirit. St Paul said, "For anyone who is in Christ, there is a new creation" (2 Corinthians 5:17). Christian morality can only be lived and understood by those who are open to receive from Christ the gift of the Holy Spirit. As the Catechism says, "The Spirit of the Lord gives new form to our desires, those inner movements that animate our lives."[34]

The *Theology of the Body* helps us to understand more deeply the nature of true love, because it enables us to fully appreciate the dignity of the human body. All love is expressed through the body and therefore, without a proper understanding of the body, we cannot have a proper understanding of love. Sadly in our culture the beautiful phrase "making love" is very often divorced from the one thing that makes sexual love true and beautiful, namely, commitment, self-giving, seeking the good of the other and openness to the gift of life. The phrase, "making love" accurately expresses the tenderness and intimacy experienced in the intimate sexual embrace in marriage. As we have seen, the sexual union between husband and wife is the holiest, the most wholesome expression of love. Their sexual union is infused with joy and pleasure, healing and reconciliation, symbolising the union of Christ and the Church. That is why we call marriage a sacrament: an outward sign of

---

[32] *Constitution on the Church in the Modern World*, 22.

[33] *Veritatis Splendor*, 103.

[34] *Catechism of the Catholic Church*, 2764.

inward grace. Sexual intercourse in marriage is truly "making love", living out the love and the grace of marriage.

Human nature not culture

In the Catholic perspective, God created sex for the very specific function of the two becoming one flesh and being fruitful in new life. This doesn't change because a cultural shift in the 1960s and 1970s introduced an acceptance and even promotion of promiscuity. The sexual "revolution" promised fulfilment but many historians, anthropologists, sociologists and theologians now believe that society is paying an extremely high price for sexual "liberation", in terms of high divorce rates, abortion rates and sexually transmitted diseases that have devastating consequences. The revolution may have introduced a cultural change in what was socially accepted sexual behaviour, but it didn't change human nature. Even the great "sex symbol", Raquel Welch, recently deplored what has happened:

> Seriously, folks, if an aging sex symbol like me starts waving the red flag of caution over how low moral standards have plummeted, you know it's gotta be pretty bad. In fact, it's precisely because of the sexy image I've had that it's important for me to speak up and say: Come on girls! Time to pull up our socks![35]

Ultimately what is at stake here is our vision of what it means to be human and how we can live a life that fulfils the deep yearning for happiness which is in every human heart. The answer lies in more self-respect, and reclaiming the true meaning of love and of the body. In other words, the answer lies in a good theology of the body.

"Cut off from me you can do nothing" (John 15:5)

We have a vision of what it means to be human, revealed to us by God. Jesus recalled humankind to a true morality of sexual relationships when he said, "What God has united, human beings must not divide" (Matthew 19:6), and also, "If a man looks at a woman lustfully, he has already committed adultery with her in his heart" (Matthew 5:28). Lust in the heart was not of God's creation. Because of that lust, as we considered in Chapter four, the heart has become the battlefield for the goodness and holiness of the body. St John says that lust, which is, "disordered bodily desires, disordered desires of the eyes, pride in possession – is not from

---

[35] www.lifesitenews.com, accessed 12 May 2010.

the Father but is from the world" (1 John 2:16). Lust owes its origin to the original sin and disobedience of our first parents. Like a virus, it attaches itself to what is good, namely human yearning for love and communion, and distorts it. It seeks to transform the God-given desire for true self-giving love into self-seeking gratification. Ultimately it uses and abuses the other, because the urge of lust is the very opposite of love. Satisfying lust cannot create the communion of persons, because lust in its very nature is self-seeking and insatiable.

We know that without the grace of God and the power of the Holy Spirit we would not be able to live in the truth of our bodies. We depend entirely on the redemption of Christ. This redemption is effective, transforming and renewing. As Blessed John Paul said:

> Redemption is a truth, a reality, in the name of which men and women must feel themselves called, and called with effectiveness… Christ's words are not a call hurled into emptiness… The words of Christ testify that the original power (and thus also grace) of the mystery of creation becomes for each one us the power (that is, the grace) of the mystery of redemption.[36]

In the mystery of our creation God made us male and female, and it is in this that we depend entirely on the redemption of Christ. The Catechism states our faith very clearly: "Christ came to restore the original order of creation disturbed by sin."[37] Some people simply reject the notion of any disturbance. For them things may be in a bit of an evolutionary mess, but there is no need for any further explanation. They would contend that human beings are greedy, lusting for power and sexual gratification – they don't need redemption – it's just being human! All people need are laws to ensure that society remains peaceful and just. Law breakers should be punished by fines or imprisonment but there is no such thing as "redemption" or "rebirth". By contrast, the Catechism provides a clear definition of sin:

> Sin is an offence against reason, truth, and right conscience; it is a failure in genuine love for God and neighbour caused by a perverse attachment to certain goods. It wounds the nature of the person and injures human solidarity.[38]

---

[36] *Theology of the Body*, 46:5.
[37] *Catechism of the Catholic Church*, 1615.
[38] *Catechism of the Catholic Church*, 1849.

Sin is identified first of all as an offence against reason and truth. Lust in all its forms is against right reason and truth, because it treats other people as a means for personal advancement, enrichment or sexual pleasure. If it is simply part of human nature, then we are stuck with it for life. But if we see it as the fruit of human sinfulness, then we can be redeemed from it. That is what Christ has done for us. His gift of redemption brings with it the interior renewal and transformation of the heart. As the Catechism puts it: "Healing the wounds of sin, the Holy Spirit renews us interiorly through a spiritual transformation. He enlightens and strengthens us to live as 'children of the light' through all that is good and right and true."[39]

The gift of friendship

Before we can joyfully live in the truth of our body, the reality of self-giving love, we have to grow in moral maturity. This means we have to cultivate good habits or, to use the old-fashioned term – virtues – and struggle to overcome bad habits – or vices. If we drink too much, for example, we need to cut down before it affects our health and relationships. Cultivating temperance in one area has an integrating influence on personal development in every other area. The human being is a unity of body and soul. Moral growth is like spring. Once growth appears in one area, it will start to appear in others, especially in the area of human relationships.

Concepts of virtue and chastity may be old-fashioned, but that doesn't mean they are not relevant. For example, the Catechism says: "The chaste person maintains the integrity of the powers of life and love placed in him or her. This integrity ensures the unity of the person."[40] It is this integrity and unity which was so severely attacked and eroded during the 1960s and 1970s. But despite this, we can be optimistic about human nature. Indeed, the Catechism points out the "laws of growth... which progress through stages marked by imperfection and too often by sin. Men and women, day by day, build themselves up through their many free decisions; and so they know, love and accomplish moral good by stages of growth."[41] The consistent rule of moral and spiritual growth is "Start again!" No moral situation is ever hopeless because the moment one turns to Christ he is there to redeem and restore. Unmarried men and women, living the single life, can live in the full truth of their bodies and experience the love of sincere self-giving, especially in their friendships.

[39] Catechism of the Catholic Church, 1695.
[40] Catechism of the Catholic Church, 2337-8.
[41] Catechism of the Catholic Church, 2343.

As the Catechism says, "The virtue of chastity blossoms in *friendship*."[42] Through the *Theology of the Body*, John Paul has helped many men and women to resist the pressure to sexualise all relationships and find friendship. As scripture says, friends are a great gift of God:

> A loyal friend is a powerful defence:
> whoever finds one has indeed found a treasure.
> A loyal friend is something beyond price,
> there is no measuring his or her worth.
> A loyal friend is the elixir of life,
> and those who fear the Lord will find one.
> Whoever fears the Lord makes true friends,
> for as a person is, so is his or her friend too.
> (Ecclesiasticus 6:14-17)

The gift of friendship that enriches life is preserved and deepened through living that love which is a sincere gift of self. For so many people, especially so many young people, John Paul's *Theology of the Body* opens up a rich spirituality of friendship.

Challenges today

Why do spouses in a marriage often feel unloved even though they frequently have intimate sexual relationships? If the gift of self is not being offered, if they are withholding something of themselves, they are only experiencing the pleasurable sensation of sex. Without the gift of self there can be no experience of love. It is only through this, that they can enter into the communion of persons and experience the fulfilling and beatifying experience of love. Married theologians like Christopher West never tire of pointing out that the sensation of sex, no matter how pleasurable or exciting it may be, is no substitute for that total, free, fruitful and faithful gift of self that conjugal union symbolises. Blessed John Paul says:

> Purity is an *"ability" centred on the dignity of the body*, that is, on the *dignity of the person* in relation to his or her own body, to masculinity or femininity that shows itself in that body. Understood as "ability", purity is precisely an expression and fruit of life "according to the Spirit" in the full sense of the term, that is, as a new ability of the human being in whom the gift of the Holy Spirit bears fruit.[43]

---

[42] *Catechism of the Catholic Church*, 2347.
[43] *Theology of the Body*, 56:1.

106

John Paul's view that the body manifests the person has liberated many hearts from the dualistic error summed up in such phrases as, "It is only my body," or "I can do what I like with my body." These cannot withstand the truth that John Paul proclaimed: we just don't *have* bodies, we *are* our bodies; we are body-persons, embodied spirits. True love is the fruit of mature purity. Blessed John Paul teaches:

> Continence (chastity) is not limited to offering resistance against concupiscence of the flesh, but through this resistance *also opens itself to the deeper and more mature values* that are part of the spousal meaning of the body in its femininity and masculinity, as well as to the authentic freedom of the gift in the reciprocal relationship of persons.[44]

The purer the heart becomes the more sensitive the spouses become to each other's needs and the more fulfilling becomes the gift of self. Indeed John Paul can say, "Purity is the glory of the human body before God."[45]

In recent years Catholic moral teaching – including the *Theology of the Body* – has come under attach from secularist quarters. Pope Benedict famously called this attitude "a dictatorship of relativism".[46] It can be summed up in this way: believe what you like, provided you don't claim that what you believe is true! In his *Theology of the Body*, John Paul is in effect calling upon men and women, not to seek the truth in God, or in the Church's teaching, but to seek it in their own bodies. How does the love within your own heart manifest itself through your body? How do you recognise the difference between self-giving and self-seeking?

Christians have always held that, by the light of reason alone, people can discern the difference between right and wrong, between living truthfully and living a lie, between being just and unjust, between love as self-giving and lust as self-seeking. Christians also say without any hesitation that men and women cannot live the Gospel life without the grace and power of redemption. In his first encyclical letter, John Paul gave us his clear vision of what human beings need in life:

---

[44] *Theology of the Body*, 128-2.
[45] *Theology of the Body*, 57:3.
[46] *The Light of the World*, 51.

Men and women cannot live without love. They remain beings that are incomprehensible for themselves, their lives are senseless, if love is not revealed to them, if they do not encounter love, if they do not experience it and make it their own, if they do not participate intimately in it.[47]

Love is the most fundamental need of the human heart and every heart hungers for an experience of love. Without love nothing else that men and women value, such as power or riches or prestige, can make them happy. "Happiness", John Paul said, "is being rooted in Love."[48]

Many Christians believe that society is broken, not because it is bankrupt, but because human love has been fractured at the deepest level. Fixing our broken society will not happen if we cannot regain a proper sense of love. And until we have a proper understanding of what it means to be a body we will never understand the true meaning of love. John Paul said it so well: "This is *the body: a witness* to creation as a fundamental gift, and therefore a witness *to Love as the source from which this same giving springs.*"[49]

Conclusion

We began this book by reflecting on the truth that each of us can say "I am my body." Following the teaching of Blessed John Paul we have looked at this from different angles, using different theological concepts and images to grasp more clearly what it means to be a human being, a body-person. Every person has a hunger to know himself or herself. We want to know and understand ourselves and the meaning and purpose of our lives. John Paul has made it very clear that only in Christ can we receive this knowledge. That is why I close this book with these memorable words of Blessed Pope John Paul the Great, in his first encyclical to the Church:

> *Those who wish to understand themselves thoroughly... must with their unrest, uncertainty and even his weakness and sinfulness, with their life and death, draw near to Christ. They must, so to speak, enter into him with all their own self, they must "appropriate" and assimilate the whole of the reality of the Incarnation and Redemption in order to find themselves. If this profound process takes place within him, they*

---

47 *Redemptor Hominis*, 10.
48 *Theology of the Body*, 16:2.
49 *Theology of the Body*, 14:4.

then bear fruit not only of adoration of God but also of deep wonder at themselves. In reality, the name for that deep amazement at the person's worth and dignity is the Gospel, that is to say: the Good News. It is also called Christianity. This amazement determines the Church's mission in the world and, perhaps even more so, in the modern world.[50]

---

[50] *Redemptor Hominis*, 10.